PREACHING ON
GREAT THEMES

MOWBRAY SERMON OUTLINES

Series Editor: D. W. Cleverley Ford

Preaching through the Acts of the Apostles: D.W. Cleverley Ford
Preaching through the Life of Christ: D. W. Cleverley Ford
Preaching through the Prophets: John B. Taylor
Preaching through the Psalms: D. W. Cleverley Ford
Preaching through Saint Paul: Derrick Greeves
More Preaching from the New Testament: D. W. Cleverley Ford
More Preaching from the Old Testament: D. W. Cleverley Ford
Preaching on Devotional Occasions: D. W. Cleverley Ford
Preaching on Favourite Hymns: Frank Colquhoun
More Preaching on Favourite Hymns: Frank Colquhoun
Preaching on Special Occasions, Volume 1: D. W. Cleverley Ford
Preaching on Special Occasions, Volume 2: D. W. Cleverley Ford
Preaching on Special Occasions, Volume 3: Edward H. Patey
Preaching on Great Themes: D. W. Cleverley Ford

Preaching through the Christian Year:
  Volume 9: Robert Martineau
  Volume 10: Brian Hebblethwaite
  Volume 11: Peter Lee
  Volume 12: John M. Turner

Preaching at the Parish Communion:
  ASB Epistles — Sundays: Year One: Robin Osborne
  ASB Epistles — Sundays: Year Two: Dennis Runcorn
  ASB Epistles — Sundays: Year Two, Volume 2: John Vipond
  ASB Gospels — Sundays: Year One: Dennis Runcorn
  ASB Gospels — Sundays: Year Two: Raymond Wilkinson
  ASB Gospels — Sundays: Year Two, Volume 2: Peter Morris

PREACHING ON GREAT THEMES

D. W. CLEVERLEY FORD

MOWBRAY

Mowbray
A Cassell imprint
Artillery House, Artillery Row, London SWIP IRT

First published 1989

British Library Cataloguing in Publication Data

Cleverley Ford, D.W. (Douglas William)
  Preaching on great themes.
  1. Christian church. Preaching
  I. Title
  251

ISBN 0–264–67174–0

Typeset by Colset Private Limited, Singapore
Printed and bound in Great Britain by
Biddles Ltd, Guildford and King's Lynn

CONTENTS

ACKNOWLEDGEMENTS

I wish to express my appreciation of the encouragement given me by Robert Williams, formerly Editor of Mowbrays Publishing Division, to write this book.

Also of the co-operation of Miss B. L. Hodge, now living at Canterbury and formerly on the staff with me at Lambeth Palace, in preparing my manuscript for the publishers, her sixth for me.

Also for the opportunity given me for preaching some of the sermons in this book in places as various as Canterbury Cathedral; Liverpool Parish Church; St Paul's, Knightsbridge; St Mary's German Lutheran Church, London; and village churches in East Surrey.

Lingfield 1988   D. W. CLEVERLEY FORD

INTRODUCTION

The 'great themes' which this book handles are theological themes, but I refrained from incorporating the word 'theological' in the title for fear of frightening off potential readers. People, even some clergy and ministers, are afraid of theology. It sounds remote, dry, and unrelated to the affairs of everyday human existence. This idea is mistaken. Theology represents an attempt to offer an orderly account of the experience of living in the light of faith in God. It concerns us all. Theology is not exclusively the specialized preserve of academics, though the form and manner in which they commonly present it does sometimes unfortunately give that impression. Ordinary congregations need theology. They will not be grounded nor built up in Christian discipleship in ignorance of it. They must be taught, but how if theological themes are not handled in the preaching? Hence this book.

A number of themes dealt with here have been taken from the *Sunday Themes* suggested by the Alternative Service Book. Others have been sparked off by the publication *We believe in God* produced by the Church of England Doctrine Commission in 1987 which hoped that its contents would form the content of parochial preaching. This is greatly to be desired for there is good material here, but the point needs to be made that it will have to be adapted for sermons if it is to be made palatable for the average congregation. This is what I have attempted.

The Bible gives the clue to the procedure required. It does not present its doctrine of God in the form of a dissertation or treatise – who would read it if it did? – but largely as narrative. It contains story after story about people and their actions and reactions. We learn what God is like when we read of his dealings with men and women, their dealings with him, and their consequent dealings with one another.

So we discover a personal God (which is not the same as to say he is a person), and we learn of his love for mankind as well as of his justice.

Most of us are captivated by people and events, not by abstractions (which have their place but not in preaching); and if their story is narrated in memorable language as in the Bible – particularly in the Authorized Version, which is its great merit – we imbibe theology almost without knowing it.

There is work to be done in the modern pulpit for times have changed and new knowledge, especially scientific knowledge, is available. It shapes our lives. So we must review, and perhaps re-present our theology in the light of it. I have tried at least to touch on this in my book though I can claim no expertise in scientific matters. Of this however I am sure, that unless modern congregations can feel that their preacher shows himself in the pulpit to be living in the same modern world which they inhabit by indicating at least an acquaintance with scientific and modern knowledge generally they may write off his theology as antiquated and without relevance to them.

Theology, however, the Church must have, and theological preaching is the only generally practical way in which congregations are likely to receive it. For the most part their members will not read theological books, nor attend theological lectures. More is the pity no doubt, but the fact must be faced that large numbers would scarcely profit by the exercise if they did. The teaching of theology, then, through the medium of preaching is the way, calling for a discipline on the part of the preacher all its own. Theological preaching in the context of the worshipping Church is what makes for the maturity and stability of a Christian community, in the absence of which it will remain weak. The Church lives by what it believes and practises and a healthy state cannot exist unless it is theologically taught.

I ought to qualify a sentence in the first paragraph of this Introduction, namely, 'Theology represents an attempt to offer an orderly account of the experience of living in the light of faith in God'. This is true so long as it does not imply that experience is the basic priority and ultimate criterion in religion. To take this for granted is, however, almost a commonplace today, deriving from the eighteenth-century movement of thought, which came to dominate Europe, called the Enlightenment (*Aufklärung*). In theological circles Friedrich Schleiermacher (1768–1834) was the key figure and his contention was that religion is based on intuition and feeling, and is independent of all dogma. Theology then is the systematic explanation of this feeling.

This is not the interpretation I have followed in this book keen though I am not to divorce theology from experience. I regard God's action and God's speech as primary, not religious intuition. Our religious experience, as I see it, is grounded in response to God's initiative and this response is the essence of faith. Such, it seems to me, is the stand taken by the Bible. It is replete with stories of the experiences of men and women, as has been noted, but they are not accounts of man's feeling for God but stories of God addressing man in word and action. Not only in action. To that extent the almost exclusive emphasis on what was called 'salvation history' (*Heilsgeschichte*), that is God's mighty acts making for our salvation, was misplaced. God also addresses man in words interpreting his actions. He did not provide ancient Israel only with national leaders but with prophets who never tired of proclaiming 'Thus saith the Lord'.

What I wish to say therefore is that theology is an attempt at producing an orderly account of our experience of the prior word and action of God in the various and varied ways we have encountered them. This is Biblical theology in the way I have understood it in writing this book. And, if this is a true interpretation, then preaching is essential for the well-being, if not for the very life, of the Church; and by preaching I mean theological preaching, Biblical theological preaching, but related to human experience and the world in which we live today, and balanced by a proper regard for reason and tradition. The balance is important. And the aim throughout is pastoral, not academic, for preaching, properly understood, is part of the *pastoral office*.

D. W. C. F.

1. An Active God

I am the Lord, that doeth all these things.

ISAIAH 45.7 (AV)

I see that in this church you invite members of the congregation to save their old newspapers and deposit them in a specific place. They will then be sold for pulping and the money raised thereby will help the church funds. A good idea! Now I will tell you something else you might do. You might gather up all the Bibles you can find inside and outside the church and dump them too for pulping, for they will be of no more use if—note I say, *if*—we accept the assertion of some that God is not an active God. He does not do anything, he just is, in fact he is Being with a capital B. I express the matter in this (no doubt) startling fashion because if there is one conclusion even the most humble reader could deduce from the Bible it is that God is always doing things—creating, sustaining, calling to people, loving, rebuking, judging and promising; the God of the Bible is an active God, and if we are not willing for this we might as well dump our Bibles forthwith.

1. *The God who not only is but does*

Nevertheless someone has just written a book purporting to tell us what the Anglican Church will be like by about the year two thousand. One of the suggestions is that belief in an active God will no longer be part of its orthodoxy. All I can say is that if such turns out to be the case there will no longer be a Church, and for this basic reason, that it will not meet people's needs nor correspond to their experience. They are more likely to bring the Church for dumping, and keep the Bible for spiritual sustenance. I am speaking bluntly but to most of us God is of no use (O, what a way to put it!) as a mere philosophical theory of existence. We want someone to cry to when 'other helpers fail, and comforts flee'; we want to believe that God does take a hand in the affairs of the world and that chance, and worse

1

still, wicked tyrants, do not have the last word; and we can't get the conviction out of our systems that somehow Providence does operate in the affairs of men.

I have just finished reading a new and recently published life of Lord Nelson by Tom Pocock. Frail in body and slight of stature he was nevertheless dazzlingly strong in will-power, though latterly abysmally weak with Lady Hamilton. But there can be no doubt that he guaranteed the supremacy of British seapower for a hundred years and altered the face of Europe. The English went mad about him for they saw him as their saviour even before Trafalgar in 1805. I knew all this before because every Norfolk man, like me, cannot help being a little proud of Nelson the Norfolk clergyman's son. What I did not know however was the spiritual experience he underwent when returning in a ship from India, ill, depressed and utterly despairing of ever rising in his profession for he was at the bottom of the ladder. But there came what he called 'a radiant orb', an infusion of joy and confidence. There was a sudden glow of patriotism. These are his words: 'Well then, I will be a hero, and confiding in Providence, I will brave every danger.' It was an experience he never forgot. And it was not unique. Professor Hardy of the Alister Hardy Research Unit at Manchester College, Oxford has listed and described other similar experiences of prominent people. No, a belief in Providence is not simply the conviction of a few what might be called 'super-religious' individuals. Deep down there is a widespread semi-consciousness of Providence which comes out in such expressions as 'Nelson was a man raised up for the times', and 'Churchill was the deliverer destiny provided'. Belief in an active God is part of man's spiritual nature. God does things for his world and with his people, taking the initiative. This is how we see him in the Bible and it accords with what we feel.

2. *The response of faith*

Now because God is an active God certain consequences follow and one is that the heart of real religion is response. Imagine someone entering into the circumstances of your life. It could be a man or a woman, someone beautiful and attractive, or someone repulsive, or simply a man or woman with whom you have to be acquainted. Will there not have to be some kind of response, perhaps trust or even love, or disregard, even hostility? A person in your circle is not a thing that can be ignored even if you try, there has to be a reaction, there has to be a response. And God is not a thing, he is like a person though not just a person writ large. He speaks, he calls, he makes his presence felt, and not only at the great crises of our lives—birth, marriage, illness, death, but on occasions when we least expect it, he breaks in. We may cry out 'No, this is not what we want, we prefer to be left on our own'. Or we may say 'Yes'. We accept what God has done and is doing. This is the essence of faith. It may come to be a great deal else, but it is that at its root, faith is the affirming response to an active God. It is not basically a philosophical idea.

And so 'faith comes by hearing' as St Paul says (Romans 10.17) 'and hearing by the word of God'. Faith is initiated by hearing what God has done in his world and with and for his people. This is why the Bible is largely a story book. It is not a collection of theological propositions, least of all is it a presentation of philosophical abstractions. It tells what happened to Abraham, Isaac and Jacob, yes and Rebeccah and Ruth and the Virgin Mary; page after page of incidents in all of which in some way, sometimes an obscure way, the presence of God is recognized and a response made.

And then, most startling of all, God is so active (if I may put it that way) that he actually entered our world as a man among us; we call it 'The Incarnation', that is the taking of our flesh upon himself. Then people could actually see him in their midst, touch him and listen to his words. And how active he was, teaching, healing and living as the friend of sinners! They had to respond to him then. And they did. Some, alas, hated him so much because he upset the *status quo* that they got together to kill him. But some trusted their very souls to him. They said 'Yes' to Jesus of Nazareth. That response made them men and women of faith. What they had then was the beginning of real religion without which it is not real.

And so the Church's ministry *par excellence* is to preach Christ, to proclaim him by word and sacrament, Christ crucified, Christ risen and Christ who will come again—preaching for a verdict, proclaiming so as to evoke the response of faith. God takes the initiative, the Church tells the story, and we reply—this is the sequence. But it only makes sense if God really is what the Bible tells him to be—an active God.

3. *The propriety of prayer*

Another consequence also follows, practical and needful—it is right and proper to pray. Yet to do so is plainly ridiculous if God never does anything but is at best a philosophical theory of existence. But our hearts tell us, and the Bible confirms what they say, quibble maybe as often our minds do, that God hears and answers prayer. Not always in the way we ask but sometimes in a startling fashion with the result that we continue as men and women of faith.

But suppose we never pray. I do not mean out of forgetfulness or even laziness, for negligence on these grounds is at least excusable though reprehensible. I mean a refusal to pray because we are of the opinion that prayer is useless. Wouldn't that situation be like the man or woman who says of another—'Oh, it is no good asking him/her for anything, you might as well talk to a brick wall'. A deliberately prayerless person is one who dishonours God and a prayerful person is one who honours him. He recognizes that God is an active God, a God who does things, does them for people. And the more he brings before God the humblest of his needs and fears, be they never so domestic, the more he honours God, for he shows that God is concerned with the humblest and lowliest; there is nothing too small or too great for his compassionate concern.

There came a day in the chequered history of the Hebrew people as recorded in the Bible when the cream of the nation was languishing in exile far from home. The land where they were settled was flat and featureless and they longed for the rugged landscape and the lush pastures of their homeland. Not surprisingly they were depressed beyond measure, having no hope any more for their future or for themselves; the grip of their oppressors was like iron, they would never go free. And then a prophet arose and he saw with the clearest of vision that nothing would change these people, no, not even if their chains were cut off, unless they had a new understanding of God. We do not know his name for certain, so we call him the second Isaiah for it is in Chapters 40–55 of the book that bears this name that we find his words to this dispirited people. And here in a nutshell is what he said. God is an active God. God is not an impassive deity. He does things. So my text from Isaiah 45.7, 'I am the Lord that doeth all these things.' Such was his peroration to a statement of God's activities as of God himself speaking: 'I have called thee by thy name: I have surnamed thee, I will gird thee . . . that they may know from the rising of the sun, and from the west, that there is none beside me. I am the Lord, and there is none else . . . I am the Lord that *doeth all these things.*'

So when you bring your old newspapers for the parish collection, see that no Bible is in the pile. You need the Bible. I need the Bible to strengthen belief in an active God, in whom we can trust and to whom we can pray. Everything worthwhile in our religion depends on this belief. God is not only the one who is, he is the one who also does.

2. The World God Made

God saw all that he had made, and it was very good.

GENESIS 1.31 (NEB)

Some years ago I had a friend who tried hard to encourage me to paint—even going to the extent of buying me a box of paints, brushes, special paper and a bottle in which to carry the necessary water. To please her I 'had a go', but I wasn't very successful. All the equipment was soon stowed away and has remained stowed away for years. Then the other day I retrieved it, and actually painted a picture. The very few people to whom I showed it said it wasn't bad, at least they recognized the subject! All the same I know I shall never be an artist in water colours, but this I have discovered. Since trying to paint I see things as I have never seen them before; colour, the effect of light, shadows, reflection in water, the changing sky; and I begin to appreciate other people's paintings and what they have achieved. In short I have learned how to see.

1. *Not a scientific account*

This morning I would like us to learn how to see the first page of the Bible, Genesis Chapter 1. Making this attempt is not an idiosyncrasy of mine. On at least one Sunday of the year, whether we use the Book of Common Prayer or the Alternative Service Book, we are required to consider the creation story; Septuagesima Sunday in the old book,

5

the ninth Sunday before Christmas in the new. Many of us unfortunately run into a great deal of trouble with this creation story, not least because we will persist in seeing it as a scientific account of how the world started, and it isn't that at all. I would like us to see it instead as a careful statement about God. In other words what we have in Genesis is not physics, and outmoded physics at that, but theology. On the first page of the Bible we are introduced to the God who will dominate the whole book from beginning to end. The Bible is about God and our relationship to him.

2. *A theological statement*

What then does the creation story in Genesis 1 tell us about God? Three things—and if anyone charges me with having taken them from von Rad's commentary I shall not mind for it would be difficult to find an exposition more profound than his. Here they are. First, the world is distinct from God; second, the world belongs to God; third, God values everything there is in the world. Yes, indeed the Genesis account is concerned with the physical world; but only in so far as the created order throws light on the creator. If you wish to learn how the world started and what are the origins of the human species, it is to physics, palaeontology, biology and a number of other scientific pursuits you must turn. Genesis knows nothing of the gigantic nuclear fission which produced the stars and the DNA responsible for the formation of the human species; but it has a distinct message about God which it is to our advantage to grasp.

(a) First then, see from Genesis 1 how *the world is distinct from God*. 'Of course', you say, 'whoever thought it otherwise?' But people did when Genesis Chapter 1 was written (about the sixth century BC), and in some ways still do, as I shall say in a minute. Nature *itself* was reverenced as divine: there is a life principle within it, visibly operative in human procreation, and not only there. So in the ancient world sex symbols were prominent in worship, notably the Baal and Asherah in the Canaanite religion which Israel was taught to reject. Also the sun, moon and stars were reverenced as gods and god-desses, the latter even controlling the destinies of men and women. God definitely was not distinct from nature and nature from God.

The philosophical presentation of this way of thinking was made famous by the seventeenth-century Portuguese Jew of Amsterdam called Spinoza. God, he said, in effect is a prevading presence within the universe and in no way beyond it. This philosophy is called Pantheism and forms the basis of much modern rationalism, and is the underlying assumption of much contemporary poetry. Nature is God and God is nature.

Post-Christian Europe however has gone on almost to banish the idea of God as Transcendent Being altogether. This world is all there is and we must make the best of it. Nevertheless the longing for 'something beyond' will not altogether lie down in the human heart and so we see modern man running after the idols of money, sex, lotteries, lucky charms and horoscopes.

Genesis 1, which I repeat is theology not science, slashes into all this with its uncompromising 'In the beginning God made the heavens and the earth'; yes, sun, moon and stars, putting the stars last almost as an afterthought in the Hebrew text, thus downgrading their divinity to the bottom. How the readers of this chapter must have reeled when they first saw it in the sixth century BC! and how cutting it still is today! The world however beautiful, however intricate, is not God, and nothing in it is divine, not even procreative sex. God is distinct from the world. The Christian faith rests on this premise. This is why the Alternative Service Book makes us read Genesis 1 at the start of every Christian year.

(b) Secondly, see from Genesis 1 how *the world belongs to God*. If we believe this we shall adopt a different attitude to nature—and this includes animals—than is the case if it does not enter our thinking at all.

I remember once being put to a considerable inconvenience because my car had broken down. I had to journey to a distant place and I did not see how I could accomplish this without a car. But I was lent one. It belonged to someone whom I greatly respected. You will understand me if I tell you the care I took of that car. I ran no risks with it in the London traffic, I did not overdrive it on the derestricted roads in the country and thus strain the engine. I did not leave it out where vandals might damage it. All this because I was acutely aware to whom the car belonged and that it was only on the road at all because its owner, and not I, had paid for it, and was continuing to pay for it.

So it is with the world of nature. If we really believe it belongs to God and it only exists because of his will and his sustaining power we shall not exploit it, nor ravish it, nor ruin it for the sake of temporary gain. Christians who take Genesis 1 seriously must be conservationists to some degree. We cannot be unconcerned about acid rain, nuclear waste, overfishing and the tearing apart of our countryside. The world, the world of nature, belongs to God and we must treat it with respect and with care. In a sense it has only been lent to our generation. We do not own it. God owns it.

(c) Thirdly, see from this chapter how *God values everything there is in the world*. Over and over again the sonorous phrase is repeated in this sonorous Genesis Chapter 1 at each stage of creation: 'And God saw that it was good'. For all the spiritual gain there is in Christian self-denial let it not spread to life-denying instead of life-affirming. This is a good world God has given us, and a beautiful world and an awe-inspiring world, let us enjoy it. 'God had given us all things richly to enjoy' is the advice given to Timothy in the New Testament (1 Tim 6.17). Of course there are rainy days and sometimes cloud and thick darkness. I know. Who doesn't know? And the volume of suffering in the world, brought so close to us now with our modern means of communication that we must either weep all day long for the sorrows of mankind or forcibly turn our heads away when we can do nothing that will avail. No individual can carry the whole world on his shoulders nor was meant to do. There is a time to weep and there is a time to laugh; and we do no honour to the Lord, the creator, if we will not rejoice when the sun shines, the flowers blossom, and we have a voice with which to sing. 'Praise the Lord, O my soul' sang the Psalmist in Psalm 104 when he recited the wonders of God's creation: 'He watereth the hills from above; the earth is filled with the fruit of thy works. He bringeth forth grass for the cattle: and green herb for the service of men; that he may bring food out of the earth, and wine that maketh glad the heart of man: and oil to make him a cheerful countenance, and bread to strengthen man's heart.'

God is distinct from the world, yes, but it does not mean he has made it and forgotten it, for it belongs to him and he sustains it as the Creator Spirit moment by moment; and he sees his handiwork as good. So should we. No, Genesis 1 is not science. Under its overall theme of creation it tells us about God, enough to make us sing 'We praise thee, O God: we acknowledge thee to be the Lord.' See it like that and we shall be seeing it as it really is, and respond with the proper attitude, thanksgiving and praise, and I hope a ready smile never far away.

3. Evolution with Faith

In the beginning God created the heaven and the earth. And the earth was waste and void; and darkness was upon the face of the deep. And the Spirit of God was moving upon the face of the waters. And God said, 'Let there be . . . and there was . . .'

GENESIS 1.1–3 (RSV)

And most of us scarcely stir in our seats when we hear it! Nor do we flinch to repeat Sunday by Sunday, 'We believe in one God the Father, the Almighty, Maker of heaven and earth, of all that is, seen and unseen'; not realizing that for some people, not least the educated young, these words tell them in no uncertain terms that church, where this sort of thing is believed, is no place for them. On the grounds of intellectual honesty they opt out. God is not the creator of the heaven and the earth.

Then we sit up, and some of us react protestingly: 'But surely there must be a God. Look at the wonders of nature—the way the humblest flower unfolds in the sunlight, the identical hexagonal pattern of every snowflake, the mystery of the birds' migratory instincts. Can you really believe that all this has come about by chance? There must be a God.'

1. *Natural selection*

Science, however, has no difficulty in pointing out that the myriad forms of life on earth have all come about by a process of adaptation to a changing environment. Adam Ford in a recent book called *Universe* gives an illustration. The moth called *Biston betularia* once had a light pattern on its wings, a protective camouflage which made it almost undetectable to birds when resting on a tree trunk. Only one in a thousand of these moths displayed a dark pattern. When, how-ever, the industrial revolution blackened the tree trunks in the

9

manufacturing Midlands with soot, the light-coloured moths had no chance to survive the onslaught of the birds when they settled on the tree trunks. Only the few dark ones survived, and within a century all the moths were seen to be dark-patterned because the breeding proceeded from them. This on a tiny scale is what has happened on a gigantic scale in the whole world of nature—and how it is we see such a variety of species of animal, plant and insect life, and why some species have entirely faded out. Adaptation to environment, or natural selection, and the survival of the fittest are the causes. The hypothesis of an original Divine Designer of the variety is unnecessary. This is the assertion.

2. *Evolution*

And so the word 'evolution' comes into play. It disturbs people who profess a religious faith, and not surprisingly. It can be disturbing. After all how can there be meaning in life, in your life or in my life if everything, including ourselves, has come about by adaptation to chance variations in the environment. If this is the truth, there can be no plan, no purpose, no future (except as a step in a process) for anything or anybody. The world is a cold, mechanical, repelling place. No wonder meaninglessness is the great threat which stands angrily over against modern man's peace of mind, and perhaps his health. If this is what the theory of evolution has produced it is not surprising that people are afraid of it.

3. *Science with faith*

But I want to present a different assessment. I want to recommend what I will call *science with faith*. I do so because I do not think the evolutionary hypothesis of the universe will be proved wholly wrong. This is why I believe there is an urgent need for science with faith; because science without faith is dangerous, and faith without science is also dangerous, though less so. The requirement therefore today is for science and faith together, each in its proper place, what I have for brevity's sake called science with faith. And it is possible now, more possible than it has been in the recent past. I say this because there are at least three ways in which a number of scientists today look at the world which make it possible. They are a new sense of awe, what is called the anthropic principle, and the law of entropy.

(a) First, *a new sense of awe*. There has of course always been a sense of awe in the face of nature—its gigantic power, its relentlessness, and the infinite variety of its forms. But the awe was largely based on ignorance. Primitive man was awestruck by the thunder clap he did not understand. What is new is the feeling of awe based on scientific knowledge.

Take the case of the atom (the word is Greek and means 'uncuttable'). The microscopic billiard-ball-like particle was accepted as the basic, irreducible constituent of all matter. But in 1911 Rutherford demonstrated how atoms consist of a nucleus orbited by electrons on the pattern of the solar system, and even the nucleus itself is composed of protons and neutrons, and they in turn of quarks and gluons. And as if this is not enough to bewilder our imagination, even these subatomic particles are but manifestations of energy, for this is what matter is—concretizations of energy. So there is mystery at the heart of the matter, not asserted on a basis of ignorance but on the most advanced scientific investigation. No wonder scientists stand in awe at what they perceive, and there is a new humility abroad in the face of ultimate reality. Not that science has proved the existence of God, it cannot, but the way is wide open now for thinking men and women to hold such a faith, and there are top-ranking scientists ready to confess it.

(b) And now, secondly, what is called the *anthropic principle* also encouraging faith in place of a soul-crippling meaninglessness. This principle puts forward the idea that the age-long development of the universe from what scientists call the 'Big Bang', and matter condensing into galaxies and stars, and producing elements such as carbon and iron, necessary for life; and precisely the right proportions of helium and hydrogen so that water could be produced; and an exact proximity and remoteness of our sun to our earth—all the fantastic evolution producing also you and me—all this in order to make possible human beings on the earth—this is the anthropic principle. Scientists are reluctant to employ the word 'purpose' but are ready to assert that the world has so evolved as to have the capacity to sustain human beings.

We must never forget that there is nothing more wonderful than a

11

human being; no computer, however sophisticated, rivals his brain; no living creature is so complex, so baffling to understand—how for instance mind has developed from matter. There is mystery here but not meaninglessness if we are willing to take the leap of faith and believe that God is in the evolutionary process. His purpose was, and is, to bring forth men and women capable of responding to him in an act of free will. To such a faith the anthropic principle lends encouragement.

(c) Thirdly, and very briefly, *the law of entropy*. What this covers is the way in which everything in the world runs down eventually to chaos and disorder. Our shoes wear out, the garden untended becomes a wilderness, civilization crumbles. On the same pattern the whole universe by crunch or decay will ultimately perish. There is, however, one place and one place only where the law of entropy is thwarted, if not reversed—the mind of man. Man is able to bring order out of chaos and to arrest decay. Is this then the reason why God's purpose has been through the evolutionary process to bring forth man? And suppose we dare to believe in the resurrection of the man Jesus, and in our own resurrection beyond the dissolution and chaos of death, do not the heavy clouds of meaninglessness begin to lift from our puzzling world and our place in it? The law of entropy has not the final word, the anthropic principle points beyond it, it points to the reasonableness of faith.

4. *An appeal for faith*

Has all this, with its technical terms, been difficult to follow? Are there not concerns for most of us closer than the workings of the evolutionary process and the structure of atoms? Not many of us are kept awake at nights worrying over these matters. Our mortgage payments, some business deal or which school to send the children to are far more problematical for us. But I have had in mind those, be they many or few, who think that science has banished faith. This is not so. We need science and we need faith, reasonable faith. We need it for our welfare, not only for our spiritual and individual welfare, but for our physical and communal welfare as well. Here are some words of Thomas Carlyle writing about France in the years 1744–1777, that is before the French Revolution, taken from his three volumes which bear that title. 'Here, indeed, lies properly the cardinal symptom of the whole widespread malady. Faith is gone out; Scepticism is come in. Evil abounds and accumulates; no man has faith to withstand it, to amend it, to begin by amending himself; it must ever go on accumulating.' Please God this is not true of our country today, but who is there who cannot help wondering? Who is there who does not see the need for the re-establishing of faith in our scientific age? This is why I have preached this difficult sermon.

4. Original Sin

I discover this principle, then: that when I want to do the right, only the wrong is within my reach.

ROMANS 7.21 (NEB)

I wonder if you are one of those people who enjoys 'throwing a spanner in the works'? There are such people around and if you are one of them—and I do not grudge the fun you derive from the exercise if that is what you like, though I do not care for it myself—let me tell you a place where you might perform. Turn up at a Leftist political meeting, or it need not even be political, any meeting motivated by what is called 'progressive thinking' will do, and stoutly affirm a belief in original sin. You will certainly put 'a cat among the pigeons', but even more likely is it that you will be hounded down as either incurably daft or downright wicked, someone who ought not to be let loose in civilized and compassionate society.

So where does the Christian go from here? The Church down the ages certainly believes in the empirical fact of original sin, and it will not first of all run to ancient dogma to substantiate its belief, but simply say, 'Look around you'. Clearly, however, the prime necessity is for us as Christians to examine the subject to discover exactly what it says, and what it does not say.

1. *Partial but permanent defect*

First of all let the point be firmly made, the doctrine of original sin does not maintain that men and women are thoroughly bad with no part good. How could it advocate such nonsense when the Bible

13

categorically affirms that man is made in the likeness of God; and for fear of misunderstanding let me quote the passage from Genesis 1.27: 'So God created man in his own image, in the image of God created he him, male and female created he them.' Which being the case we cannot possibly run away with the idea that man is basically corrupt. How could he be if he is made like God? God is not corrupt! Moreover, quite apart from the Bible, commonsense ought to tell us that we could not even discuss goodness if, being totally corrupt, we had no goodness in us. We would not even know what we were talking about! So that whatever original sin means it certainly does not mean that we are all basically bad.

But what about this phrase 'made in the image of God'? Granted we are not naturally bad but are we naturally good? That is to say, do we, do all of us, does everyone tend towards goodness? Or to put the matter another way; we may not be like God now, but are we gods in the making? Are we 'unfinished', so to speak; and given time and given the right circumstances, shall we, being basically good, develop excellent characters and outstanding achievements admittedly not currently observable beyond those we recognize? In the end will all be well because man is basically sound, and Utopia not a wild dream, but a future inherent in the very nature of man—or to employ a technical word—his perfectibility?

I am asking hard questions and maybe we would like to dodge them, but can we? Here are two men arguing politics for all they are worth, perhaps on your doorstep. Both are confident that they have the right policies for improving the life of the community, but one is more cautious. He is keen enough on his programme for the future but is careful not to expect too much of human nature, and is also alive to the possibility of any plan, however sound, being twisted for personal gain. The other man, for his part, pays scant attention to the weaknesses in human nature; given the right circumstances, produced by the right policies, they will correct themselves. What is the difference between these two men? Is it not that the first is conscious of original sin although he might not use this phrase or even know it, and the second discounts it? If both happened to be philosophers, the one would look to St Augustine, the other to Jean-Jacques Rousseau and be known as 'a progressive'.

So we can't dodge this doctrine of original sin but we had better understand what it says and does not say. The river of human nature is not solid mud, or to use an old-fashioned phrase 'totally depraved', but it is *muddy* and will not clean itself. We shall be wise to come to terms with this fact, not least in our political programmes.

2. *The bondage of the will*

And now this word 'original'. Why *'original'* sin? What does this mean—that we are all born sinners? Does it mean that we are tainted from the start? Does it mean that we are dubbed guilty even before we begin living our lives, guilty from the cradle? Even worse, does the phrase 'original sin' declare that we all merit damnation, and that the whole human race is concluded under judgement whatever good deeds we manage to accomplish?

This is terrible, and the more terrible fact is that people have believed this, and acted in the light of this belief, even drawing up a fierce, repulsive, threatening religion with this as a basis. Is it surprising that loud protests are voiced? Why should innocent babies be damned? And is it surprising that good men and women have gone off into atheism because of this doctrine? And we have to concede that the great Augustine himself cannot be let off the hook of responsibility for this shocking idea of inherited guilt.

What I have to make clear is that this interpretation of original sin is a vast mistake. I know, of course, that it has been built up on the story of Adam and Eve in the garden of Eden in Genesis Chapter 3, but that chapter does not record history, it is a dramatization in picture form of *a present reality*. Adam and Eve stand for you and me now. No, what original sin proclaims is the truth that we are all bound together in the bundle of life, what theologians call 'the solidarity of mankind'. None of us starts with a clean slate. On the contrary every one of us is born into a complex of factors—genetic, historical and social, through inheritance, environment and much else. Every child is conditioned from birth and goes on being conditioned. And aggression and self-assertion are endemic to every living creature, including humans, indeed often most cruel in humans. They are instinctively part of the thrust of life.

What all this adds up to is the recognition that no one is solely and wholly responsible for the way he or she acts. And also why it is harder to do good than to do evil. Here also is the reason for tempering the harshness of our judgement upon people's individual

15

sins. Our wills are not wholly free. We cannot always do the good we would like to do. Our wills are in fact half in bondage. So my text from St Paul's own experience, 'I discover this principle, then: that when I want to do the right, only the wrong is within my reach.' This is what the doctrine of original sin is all about, and put like this, you will see that far from being a harsh judgement, it is the complete opposite. It recognizes the human predicament, the human tragedy—basically good people, made in the image of God, caught in a network of contingencies which does not leave their wills, no, *our* wills, wholly free. We are all in the same boat. This, I repeat, is the human predicament.

3. *Christ the liberator*

What then is the way out? How can we become free? free to do what we recognize to be right? free to achieve what we would like to achieve but cannot? And let us be quite clear what we are talking about—freedom of the will.

There was a news item on sound radio the other day about a Yorkshireman, a chain smoker who longed to be free of the habit but couldn't break it. So in desperation he betook himself to a small uninhabited island off the West coast of Scotland taking with him, we were told, only a few books and a bottle of whisky (though surely he must have had some sandwiches!). Obviously there were no cigarettes, and no other people from whom either to borrow or purchase them; not even a boat called at the place. We were never informed if he succeeded with his plan, but clearly what he was attempting was to break a weak will by the exercise of one strong act of will, one would have to say a desperate act of will.

But we can't take this as a model. We can't escape original sin by going anywhere. And if some sort of moral paradise did exist in some place, a beneficent Utopia, we should take our selves with us and quickly spoil it. And who in his senses imagines we should all be stronger in will if we lived in the sunshine of a *Costa del Sol* all day and every day, and with an unlimited cash supply? Read the recently published story of the Woolworth heiress, *Poor Little Rich Girl*, if that is what you think! And what about a vastly improved educational system? or an extended health service? or full employment with no possibility of inability to find work?—all eminently desirable no doubt—but would the human problem be solved? That is the question. Would we be better people thereby?

Take this human predicament to heart and you will feel for St Paul's *cri de coeur* in Romans 7.24, 'Who is there to rescue me out of this body doomed to death?' He summed it up in his earlier words (our text for today), 'I discover this principle, then: that when I want to do the right, only the wrong is within my reach.' And then firmly he provides the answer: 'God alone, through Jesus Christ our Lord! Thanks be to God!'

And maybe we shrug our shoulders. But we wouldn't if we had had the experience of opening our hearts to Christ, and our minds. We would have discovered that in a faith-allegiance to him we could do, albeit with stumbling, what otherwise we could never do. Or as we have it in the words of Christ himself as given in John 8.36, 'If then the Son sets you free, you will indeed be free.'

5. The Election of God's People: Abraham

Now the Lord said unto Abram, Get thee out of thy country, and from thy kindred, and from thy father's house, unto the land that I will shew thee: and I will make of thee a great nation, and I will bless thee, and make thy name great; and be thou a blessing.

GENESIS 12.1–2 (RV)

Last December an article in the *Reader's Digest* about Mother Teresa, 'the living saint of Calcutta', caught my attention. It told of the extraordinary growth of her work—how in forty years the religious order she founded had grown from a membership of one to some three thousand sisters and four hundred brothers, all at a time when many similar orders are declining; and how there are branches of her work in many countries of the world now; and how in 1979 she was awarded the Nobel Peace Prize. What captivated me in the article however was the impression she made on entering a soup kitchen in Kilburn, NW London, where one hundred and twenty tattered men and women were seated waiting to be fed at long trestle tables in what could only be described as a Dickensian scene. Her sudden appearance in the doorway was as if someone had switched on a light.

There she was, aged seventy-seven, bent, wrinkled and obviously very tired, dropping in on her way from Moscow to Rome, large work-worn hands and big feet, a tiny creature only five feet tall, of Albanian descent. How is this extraordinary woman to be accounted for? Surely no answer will suffice except that she believes in God, and lives so close to God that his love shines out of her eyes motivating her whole being. What is more, in and through her thousands of otherwise hopeless people have been blessed.

1. God works through people

This is how God works. He chooses people, most often very ordinary people, ordinary looking, ordinary in personality, but they believe in God, believe in him notwithstanding their own faults and failings, believe in him implicitly, that is to say trust him with their whole past, present and future; and the outcome is extraordinary. Mother Teresa is one such in our day and generation, George Müller, Hudson Taylor and Pastor Bodelschwingh of Bethel in Germany, were others in the last century. The main fact about them, however, is not what they became in themselves, but what they did for other people. It is no exaggeration to say that thousands upon thousands were lifted up through these men of faith to a worthwhile life, having possessed nothing worthy of the name. This is how God works. He chooses people, and, when they respond by trusting him, his beneficence is spread abroad.

This principle of divine operation is introduced in the very first book of the Bible in the story of Abraham (or Abram to be more accurate at this stage). 'Now the Lord said to Abram, Get thee out of thy country, and from thy kindred, and from thy father's house, unto the land that I will shew thee: and I will make of thee a great nation, and I will bless thee, and make thy name great; and be thou a blessing.' And Abraham did just that. He went out from the comfortable and settled life of Ur of the Chaldees to become a wandering sheikh in the desert with no other assurance than his faith that what God had promised he would provide. Abraham thus became a pioneer in faith-living, and as such the father of all the faithful down the centuries who have trusted God implicitly.

2. *Breaking with the past*

We ought to concentrate for a moment on Abraham's leaving of his familiar background and stepping out into the unknown, out into the desert. Such religion as he possessed—and all the ancients held to a religion of some kind—would largely be based on fear, fear of god or of gods who needed to be propitiated constantly, else they would react with fierce anger, visiting the earth with terrible catastrophes and people with terrible diseases, as often as not crowned with an untimely, if not hideous death. All the rituals and taboos which buttressed their lives were directed at deflecting the deadly evils which perpetually hovered in the shadows. All this was the dark backcloth of Abraham's ideology and the controller of the cultural setting in which he passed his days.

The beginning of his greatness came when he broke from all this, and from his contemporaries who hung on to it, and trekked out into the desert alone at the instigation of what he believed was a call from the Great Unknown. Did the hot, burning sun shimmering across the sands emphasize his puny strength? Did the stars in the night sky, hanging like great lamps, dwarf him in the presence of this immensity of space? But out there an extraordinary revelation came to him, he became conscious of God not as his enemy but as his friend, not a frightening force ready to crush him on the flimsiest whim, but someone who actually cared for him and wished to prosper him. And wonder of wonders, he believed that this was the *nature* of God, and this God he took the step of trusting implicitly, trusting with his entire life and destiny. It is this faith which gives Abraham his mighty stature in the whole history of mankind. His faith in the God who cares made him what he came to be, the father of the men and women of faith for all time.

We must not overlook the necessity of the break with the past in order to rise to the stature of dynamic faith. All the old mumbo-jumbo of fetishes, lucky charms, lucky stars and fortune-telling has to go, or at least be treated as foolish fun. Belief in an absentee God has to go, a God who created the world and then forgot about it, or let it go on running by itself like a car till it ran out of petrol. Belief too in a God who does not know the meaning of suffering, a God whose heart is not touched by calamities wrecking the lives of the innocent, but who sits enthroned in splendour like some callous potentate; yes, and

19

the Unmoved Mover of the Universe some philosophers have proclaimed. And of course a vindictive God who hits out when we displease him but can be bought off with piety and rituals. All this has to go. We cannot be men and women of faith in the true God so long as we cling to this old background, and without faith in the great God who humbled himself in Christ because he cares for us, without this faith, I repeat, we shall never achieve our full potentiality.

3. *Faith does not make us perfect*

Come back to Abraham. He did cut with the past and all its heathen trappings. He did march out into the desert with no other security for the future but his confidence in the God he believed was his friend. But none of this heroic action turned him into a saint overnight, using that word 'saint' in the popular sense. He in fact stumbled into foolishness and doubt; but God did not desert him. I find this most encouraging.

There came a day—the story is told in this very same Chapter 12 of Genesis where Abraham made his great act of faith—there came a day when he went down into Egypt on account of a famine, and played there a mean little trick designed to save his own skin. It didn't work and he was made to look foolish. This was the trick. He instructed his beautiful wife, Sarah, to announce that she was his sister; then the Egyptians would not kill him to get 'this beauty' for themselves. So they did not kill him but they did take Sarah, in fact Pharaoh took her into his own house and paid Abraham handsomely for the prize. All very sordid. And the truth came out. Sarah was Abraham's wife, not his sister. It is a wonder Pharaoh did not kill him for this trick; instead he sent Sarah back home to Abraham making himself look the better man. So where was Abraham's faith in God now? Where indeed?—badly bruised and broken; but do not miss the point: even though Abraham was temporarily faithless, God remained faithful. He preserved his servant in danger from Pharaoh.

And here is another story. God had promised Abraham and Sarah a son. Of this Abraham was convinced, but Sarah doubted, and not surprisingly on account of her age. So they decided to help God keep his promise! What naivety! Abraham should take a mistress, or concubine to use the old phraseology. And he got her with child. Where then was Abraham's faith in God? Where indeed? And troubles arose. They usually do where wives and mistresses are involved. Sarah was jealous and the mistress had to flee the house. And if you want to read about love look up Genesis Chapter 21 and see Abraham up early in the morning with bread and a bottle of water because he could not bear to think of the girl thrust out into the desert with nothing. How mixed up all this is! How commonplace! How far removed from implicit faith in God. But once again God was faithful. Abraham was not cast off. Sarah did bear a son and Abraham rose to a monumental faith again when he showed himself willing to sacrifice that son if this was what God required.

I tell you, I find enormous comfort here. God will never desert us even though at times we make a mess of our faith. God always stays faithful to his chosen servants.

4. *Election for service*

I can't tell you why some men, some women are chosen to be shining examples of faith despite the cracks in it. I don't know. No one knows. But this I do know, they are not chosen simply for their own happiness, even though happiness attends their lives. God chooses people so that through those men and women of faith thousands of others may be blessed.

Abraham grasped the message. He looked up at the stars and heard God's promise that his descendants would be as numerous. An overstatement? Yes, very likely when taken literally but the implication was sure. The men and women who, in ages to come, would follow in the footsteps of his faith in God as a friend would equal the stars of heaven for multitude, and through those people the world would be blessed. This has happened.

The whole Hebrew nation was chosen for this kind of caring service. Its people were God's chosen people and Abraham was their father. Were they consistently faithful? But what right has the Church to throw stones? For let us be well assured, the Church is God's chosen people for that brand of service, proclaiming and demonstrating the love of God for all people everywhere, especially the outcast, diseased and impoverished. The Church is God's faithful servant when it ministers wholeness to those in need, whether bodily or spiritual, or, as is usual, both together.

Election for service then, not for privilege. It is at this point that the doctrine of predestination went wrong with its terrible teaching of a few predestined for salvation and a vast majority predestined for damnation. No, election is for service; and Abraham is the patriarch, in the following of whom are all those down the ages who through their faith have been, and are, a blessing to others, be it to one solitary needy individual or to a thousand. Hear then the great text on faith again and what it means in practice: 'Now the Lord said unto Abram, Get thee out of thy country, and from thy kindred, and from thy father's house, unto the land that I will shew thee: and I will make of thee a great nation, and I will bless thee, and make thy name great; and be thou a blessing.'

This is how God works, he still does.

6. Do Not Dethrone Moses

In thy commandments I find continuing delight;
I love them with all my heart.

PSALM 119.47 (NEB)

Moses is not very popular these days. I do not mean the man Moses. How could he be popular? He lived at least three thousand years ago and didn't speak English. I mean that for which Moses stands, what he embodies in himself, that is, rules for successfully living together in a community. We don't like rules. We all want to be free, free to 'do our own thing', free to express our individuality, free to do what we wish to do without let or hindrance from any outsider. Discipline and authority are 'old hat' since the 1960s. I repeat Moses is not very popular these days. And yet he was the man who led the Hebrews out of the slavery of Egypt into the freedom of what was called 'the promised land'. But he also insisted that no nation, no community is able to hold together without a generally accepted code of behaviour. Liberty and equality do not of themselves make for fraternity. There have to be rules to sustain freedom. That is the bit we do not like but that is the bit for which Moses stands.

1. *Moses the man*

But who was this Moses? Why should we listen to him? Moses stands as the second great man in the Old Testament, Abraham being the first. Abraham founded a family, Moses founded a nation. Abraham was a lonely figure in his time, pushing out on his own into the future; Moses stands always at the head of a crowd shaping it into a nation. Abraham is conspicuous for his faith, Moses for the laws he gave the community for successful living. You can't start without faith. You can't mature without discipline. So they come in this order. First Abraham, then Moses. We shall be wise to learn of both in turn.

Who was this Moses? Moses was a giant, a giant as a leader. He was one of those men who rise to the top not because they are geniuses in one field of activity but because they are far above the average in many fields of activity. This is the qualification for leadership on a grand scale: excellence as an all-rounder. With this composite qualification the leader has touch with many *different* people at many different points, and so is able to grasp the whole. For a potential leader to possess only one outstanding skill, be it as a scientist, artist or musician, is to be in for failure. Contact will be lacking with large sections of the led. Neither can he ostensibly belong exclusively to one cultural level; he must have a sympathetic rapport with human beings as human beings at all levels whatever their attainments or lack of attainments. Both Wellington and Napoleon excelled in this. The best is for the leader to know from personal experience how it feels to face danger, what it is like to be a fugitive on the roads; yes, and to live close to kings and queens, to rub shoulders with prisoners, to hear the voice of God calling when 'nothing seems to add up'; to be physically strong, mentally alert and well-informed, and resolute of will; someone who can stand alone in the blazing sun or the pitch blackness of the night; and dare I say it?, someone physically striking. Get all this in our sights and we have some idea of the stature of Moses. He was a giant.

2. *Moses—the instrument of God*

Now I have got myself in a tangle in this sermon and I shall have to extricate myself speedily or I shall make matters worse. I have been giving the impression that we ought to listen to Moses, and the laws for which he stands because he was a giant of a man, and so he was. But there have been other giants around, and not all of them in the remote past as is the case with Moses three thousand years ago, so why listen to *him*? Of course the ten commandments are attached to his name, but did they not originate in the need to regulate the lives of some half-savage Semitic tribes by adapting a set of current taboos? What have they to do with the twentieth century?

If it didn't sound so silly I should feel tempted to say that the Bible, and the scripture where we read of Moses and the ten commandments, were aware that these doubts would be raised, and so prefaced the account with the statement, Exodus 20.1 (NEB), '*God* spoke, and these were his words'. Maybe, however, we twentieth-century people find it difficult to accept the idea of Moses cutting two tablets of stone, as we are told in Exodus 34, and God writing the ten commandments on them. I, too, am a twentieth-century man. So we shall probably have to say something like this: as Moses was formulating these laws for the Hebrew people he knew within himself that they represented the mind and will of God. In this way the ten commandments are God's commandments, not merely Mosaic commandments, giant though he was. He was acting by God's choice as God's instrument for his purpose, in which case we had better listen even though the utterance was three thousand years ago. And for this reason, that it shows how in the mind of God any community is to be held together as a community. Rules are essential, rules freely accepted, for without rules disintegration results. And note, not many rules, but very few, and very plain. Thus understood, the ten commandments are a divine gift to mankind to preserve the good of living together safely.

And please note, God did not promulgate the commandments in Egypt but at Sinai. Never under slavery did Moses promote them by promising freedom if the Hebrews obeyed them. No, first God, through Moses, gave freedom; then he taught them how to safeguard that freedom by providing rules for living. Yet still in our day, people will persist in imagining that first God provides rules and then, if we keep them, he will reward us with salvation; whereas of course the truth is the other way round. First salvation is wrought for us by Christ's cross and resurrection, then he shows us how to safeguard it.

3. *Commandments for God's people*

The ten commandments then are primarily for God's redeemed people, by which the newly-found nation come out of Egypt would be stabilized as a nation, preserve its identity and overcome opposition. The commandments were seen therefore not only as *a way of life*, a life-style peculiar to Israel, but joyfully accepted as the instrument of the nation's very life itself. The nation lived because it kept the commandments. And expanded into what the Hebrews called the *Torah* (the Hebrew word for law), it was no harsh, dull repressive thing. On the contrary it was something to quicken the heart, a gift from God for which to praise him. Hence almost the whole of the longest Psalm, number 119, concerned with the *Torah*, is joyful and is epitomized in the text I have chosen for this sermon: 'In thy commandments I find continuing delight; I love them with all my heart.'

Was there a time in the Church of England when we appreciated this; a period when we were aware that the commandments were not a whip, nor an instrument of repression but given in order that God's people should preserve their salvation and its wholesomeness, and safeguard their identity? Is this why the commandments used to be displayed prominently on the east wall of the church building, most likely on the reredos along with the Apostles' Creed and the Lord's Prayer? This, the display said in effect, is what the Church believes; this is how the Church prays; and this (the ten commandments) is how the Church conducts itself in the world, in default of which it possesses no distinctive identity, and very little future. In a number of churches in the City of London built by Wren, this display can still be seen.

4. *Commandments for the community*

I said just now that the commandments were for God's people, God's redeemed people, to preserve the life they had been given. This does not mean that they have no bearing on the community or the nation as a whole. But we cannot *require* their observance by the general public. We cannot enforce them by law. Not that we enforce them in the Church, but we cannot even display them in the Town Hall as we do in church. Even so the community would be wise to observe them if it

25

would save itself from disintegration. It cannot continue wholesome if it does not take the ten commandments as the elementary rules of corporate human life. You shall not kill. You shall not commit adultery. You shall not steal. It is to be wondered if community life is not failing in Britain today partly for this very reason, that we have discounted the validity of what is really the Magna Charta for the human race. We have terrorism on our streets. We do not simply excuse adultery, we advertise it, even recommend it. And as for stealing, the losses incurred in business are colossal and all but crippling. When shall we learn that the way of the commandments is the way of success and joy in living together? No, we cannot *command* the community to live by them, but the community would be wise to pay attention, and maybe to begin by ceasing to treat them as a joke.

I began this sermon by saying that discipline and authority are 'old hat' since the 1960s. Maybe this is still largely true but I fancy I see a slight turn of the tide, beginning with the young, beginning in some schools. I read of pupils becoming wearied with unruliness. It is ruining their chances of achievement in a competitive world. It is therefore spoiling their sense of satisfaction. And they see for themselves how not even a game can be played unless there are rules and the players agree to abide by them. And no club, not even a boys' club or a girls' club can exist without rules. What is more the adults in charge of them, and this includes parents, actually confer a boon on the young when they supply them with instructions which they must obey. I recall when I lived in Hampstead that distinguished principal of Westfield College, Mrs (later Baroness) Stocks, stressing how much easier parents made it for their adolescent girls when they set a strict time by which they must be in at night. The decision was not left to the girls and therefore they were not laughed at by some others. Yes, there are ways in which rules make life easier as well as more successful. When shall we learn in Britain so to view the ten commandments? Perhaps more than we think, our survival as a community depends on the answer we give to this basic question. So don't dethrone Moses.

7. The Remnant of Israel

. . . looking unto Jesus the author and perfecter of our faith.

HEBREWS 12.2 (RV)

You will see from the typed notice paper distributed in the church [St Peter and St Paul, Lingfield, Surrey] week by week that the theme for this Sunday's worship following the Alternative Service Book is 'The Remnant of Israel'. I wonder what you made of it? Does it refer to a length of material, say of cotton, wool or terylene? Does it conjure up pictures of an excursion to the draper's store in order to purchase some fabric for new chair covers or curtains; and when your eye lights on something you really like, the saleswoman replies, 'I am sorry there isn't enough of this material, I have only *this remnant left*'; and she holds up half a yard or half a metre, which is no use at all, you want at least twenty metres?

1. *A history lesson*

So what is this title for today, 'The Remnant of Israel'? I can tell you in a few words. Only a small proportion of the Hebrew nation called to serve God, and to worship him, stayed faithful; the great bulk drifted away. Those who did not drift away were known as 'the faithful remnant'.

Let me expand a little. God, according to the Bible, set free the Hebrew people from their bitter bondage in Egypt. He accomplished it by the leadership of that giant of a man called Moses. Not surprisingly they rejoiced in their freedom, indeed they exulted in it, and out of gratitude worshipped God, their saviour from slavery, pledging themselves to live out their lives in accordance with his will as expressed in what are called 'the ten commandments'. But in process of time they grew weary of the commandments. Most people grow weary of commandments. They restrict freedom. So, restless and irritated, these Hebrews began to grumble that they had exchanged one kind of bondage in Egypt for another kind of bondage, namely to religion. What they wanted was total freedom, freedom for everyone to do as he or she likes. So they came to hate the rules. They kicked them over. They adopted the life-style of their neighbours which seemed so free and easy. They even took over their gods. And

27

so the national religion which had given the Hebrew people distinctiveness, unity and strength, became a minority movement within the nation. Then decline set in, until in the end Israel became a prey to its enemies who overran its homeland and depopulated it, settling the skilled of the people far away in foreign exile. It was a terrible time. Only a tiny proportion of the nation ever returned to Jerusalem and Judaea; they were 'the remnant of Israel', but the rest were lost to this day, dispersed among the nations.

2. *The Church is the faithful remnant*

I have given you a little history lesson, and you may well ask what reference can all this possibly have to you? I will answer your question. I see the faithful remnant in front of me now as I stand in this pulpit, because this is what the Church is, the Church gathered round the Lord's table. It is God's faithful remnant. Only ten per cent of the population in England are church-goers and in the big cities less than one per cent. This does not mean that all the church-goers are exemplary in conduct and all the non-church-goers reprehensible. What it does mean is that the church-goers are faithful in acknowledging publicly their belief in God and his lordship over the whole of life.

There are, however, two dangers facing the faithful remnant: one is shame and the other is pride. Take shame first. Most people hate being in a minority, especially young people. There is a preference for being lost in the crowd, to be dressed like the crowd, and to speak like the crowd. Fashion is a powerful force. It shapes people, stereotypes them and dwarfs their individuality. This has a bearing on church-going. The young man or young woman in an office, or any gathering of people, does not like being set apart as a church-goer. And which of us when in company, when some disparaging remark is made about religion, has not either stayed silent or else uttered something so lame it were better not to have spoken at all? And on a housing estate, considerable courage is required for any one resident to be seen making for a church on a Sunday. Here inside the church building, when we are together, we recite the Creed with gusto—'We believe in God, the Father Almighty'—but out there when we are alone and scoffers may be around, we hide our Christian commitment, we hate being 'the faithful remnant'. We are half ashamed of it. That is one danger.

The other danger is pride, spiritual pride, pride in being different from the general run of people, many of them content to grub along with trivialities, money making, food and drink, and lurid videos. The faithful remnant which returned from exile in Babylon to Jerusalem and Judaea in the year 537 BC fell into this trap. They flaunted their differences from their heathen and irreligious neighbours. They became, in consequence, hard and narrow, even bigoted. Not all, of course, but sufficient to furnish the faithful remnant with this repelling aspect. In our Lord's day it showed up glaringly in the Pharisees. And before we write off these people, let us not forget that the Christian Church has had its periods of triumphalism, parading its sumptuous ceremonies, its splendid sanctuaries and its superb aesthetic rituals. Make no mistake the Church has contributed magnificently to the culture of Europe, but care is needed not to fall into the trap of overweening pride; it is one of the dangers confronting the faithful remnant.

So how ought we to react, faced as we are with the twin pitfalls of shame and pride? The right way is with confidence. Confidence not in ourselves as being superior persons who by our own marvellous insight have raised ourselves to a level of distinctiveness; but confidence in that we have been *given*, not earned, the faith we have, for a reason and purpose known only unto God. And we ought to remember this—that the faithful remnant, for all its imperfections and sometimes glaring faults, has nevertheless been the bearer of the sacred tradition of worship down the ages. We must not be ashamed to belong to the faithful remnant. We must not spoil our allegiance with improper pride.

3. *Jesus, the faithful remnant*

And now I would like you to visualize Jesus of Nazareth standing quite alone before Pilate, the Roman governor, in the month of April, AD 29. He was being condemned to a death he could have avoided had he been willing to compromise and close his mouth from proclaiming the truth of God. But he kept on steadily without wavering, without falling and without transgressing what God requires of every man. He

29

was 'the faithful remnant', the one wholly and completely faithful remnant, faithful unto death. Therefore God raised him from the dead, setting this seal of identity for evermore on this one man—he, Jesus of Nazareth, is Jesus the Christ, he is the Lord Jesus Christ, he is the faithful remnant.

And so we see ourselves as Church people gathered around him. Let people say if they will, 'What have you to be proud of, that you set yourselves apart?' We shall answer, 'Not much, in fact very little indeed, but look at our leader! Look at the One we follow! Look at him who is in our midst, he is our justification!' And we might, if we knew our New Testament well, recite this verse from Hebrews 12 (v. 2) quietly to ourselves: '. . . let us run with patience the race which is set before us, looking unto Jesus the author and perfecter of our faith; who for the joy that was set before him endured the cross, despising the shame, and is set down at the right hand of the throne of God.' And if we were fortunate enough to know the Greek New Testament we should reflect on that word *Archēgos*, used to describe Jesus and translated 'author' or 'captain' of our faith, but equally correctly translated as 'Prince' (see Acts 3.14). I like that. I am proud to belong to the Church of which Christ is the Prince. I hope you are too, and that neither you nor I will ever be ashamed to admit membership of *his* faithful remnant.

8. The Advent Hope

*'Keep awake, then; for you do not know on what
day your Lord is to come.'*

MATTHEW 24.42 (NEB)

I begin today with a confession; not a confession of faith but a confession of doubt. Not about the whole Christian faith, far from it, but about how to interpret the bit that is brought to our consideration on Advent Sunday, namely the Second Coming of Christ. Let me remind you of the Collect. 'Almighty God, give us grace that we may cast away the works of darkness, and put upon us the armour of light, now in the time of this mortal life, in which thy Son came to visit us in great humility; that in the last day, when he shall come again in his

30

glorious Majesty . . .' Did you hear that? Two comings! One in humility as the babe of Bethlehem (an event in history), the other, in glorious majesty (an event in the future). How are we to interpret this second coming? How and what is this to be?

Maybe you are thinking it strange to begin on this note of doubt, but I do so on purpose because I have reason to know that shared doubts can sometimes help us to shared faiths; indeed the sharing of doubts can lead to an openness and sense of understanding that leads to a renewal of faith; and few dispositions are more important.

Yes, I believe in the Second Coming of Christ. I was brought up in the Anglican church my family attended to believe in it. At the age of fifteen I knew the Greek word for it—*parousia*—as well as I knew my own name and much else besides including the details about it in the Apocalypse. What, however, came to trouble me in later years was how all this was to be interpreted. Surely not literally! 'For the Lord himself shall descend from heaven with a shout, with the voice of the archangel, and with the trump of God: and the dead in Christ shall rise first. Then we that are alive, that are left, shall together with them be caught up in the clouds, to meet the Lord in the air: and so shall we ever be with the Lord.' (1 Thessalonians 4.16, 17)

No, we can hardly accept this literally—meeting the Lord in the air!—but if on that account we reject the Advent Hope, that is, the Second Coming of Christ 'lock, stock and barrel', we shall be out of alignment with the whole New Testament, for it is embedded there and cannot be deleted without destroying the whole.

How, then, can we interpret this piece of Christian teaching? What can it say to our day and generation?

1. *God's action*

First, I suggest, that we cannot put the world right ourselves, only God can accomplish it. Certainly we can improve it and we should labour to improve it, leaving no stone unturned to upgrade the lot of men, women and children; and this includes collective and individual action, State and private enterprise, employing all the sciences and techniques of which modern man is capable. This however is the sobering truth: we shall never be able to go on with our improvements till Utopia on earth is established. A man-made Utopia there never will be.

31

Don't we know this 'in our bones' as we come to the twentieth century? We know it as our forefathers never knew it as they came to the close of the nineteenth century. Science and technology had made such rapid progress in the 1800s that a doctrine of inevitable progress was almost standard thinking, fuelled by the optimistic philosophy of the Enlightenment or *Aufklärung*, as it was called in Germany where it took so firm a hold. Even Biblical scholars conformed. No wonder they found Albert Schweitzer shocking when he insisted that the New Testament is orientated not towards man's ultimate achievement, but towards God's intervention in human history bringing it to a final climax. This is what the theologians call 'eschatology' or 'the doctrine of last things', pictured in the New Testament as the Second Coming of Christ.

Notice how I have employed the word 'picture'. Perhaps a more up-to-date word would be 'symbol'. This anyway is how I interpret the Second Advent accounts in the New Testament. I see them as pictures which convey in startling, sometimes lurid colours the message that, in the last resort, only God can right the wrongs of the world. And have we not almost come round to this ourselves from our own experience of despair? We solve one problem only to spark off another. We conquer space with air travel faster than sound and we ruin whole communities with a barrage of noise. We discover how to control agricultural pests with insecticides thus producing more food for the hungry, and we all but ruin the environment in consequence. We have instant news coverage with radio and television across the globe, and we have overburdened the human spirit with a weight of tragedies it cannot sustain.

The twentieth century has been a terrible century. No sooner was it under way than the Great War broke out bringing horrors like Verdun, the Somme and Passchendaele which have never been eradicated from the human memory. And then the Russian revolution, then the barbaric cruelties of the Nazi culture, then Hiroshima, then the overhanging threat of nuclear warfare, and now terrorism in our streets. And all the while living standards in the affluent countries have risen and are still rising. Who can sort out this bizarre tangle? The Advent message is clear if strident. No man can sort it out for he is tangled in his own soul. Only God can sort it out. This is what the doctrine of the Second Coming of Christ is crying out to say:

32

Christ has died
Christ is risen
Christ will come again.

2. *The future of the universe*

'Christ will come again.' So we speak of the Advent Hope. The message of the New Testament is not only one of despair—man cannot sort out this world—but also one of hope—God will sort it out. God has a purpose for it. It is not 'full of sound and fury signifying nothing'. Listen to this from the Epistle to the Romans, one of the great passages of the New Testament, as set out in the New English Bible. 'For I reckon that the sufferings we now endure bear no comparison with the splendour, as yet unrevealed, which is in store for us. For the created universe waits with eager expectation for God's sons to be revealed. It was made the victim of frustration, not by its own choice, but because of him who made it so; yet always there was hope, because the universe itself is to be freed from the shackles of mortality and enter upon the liberty and splendour of the children of God.'

I read in a stiff theological book the other day the suggestion that the universe never had a beginning and will never have an ending, and that the idea of God's continuous creation of the universe, that is his sustaining power of it, implies this. I think this is mistaken. God alone is without beginning and without ending. God alone is eternal. The earth and the heavens on the contrary are temporal; or, as one of the impressive Advent readings from the Old Testament expresses the contrast, 'Lift up your eyes to the heavens, and look upon the earth beneath: for the heavens shall vanish away like smoke, and the earth shall wax old like a garment, and they that dwell therein shall die in like manner; but my salvation shall be for ever, and my righteousness shall not be abolished.' (Isaiah 51.6 RV)

There is in the scriptures, it seems to me, a parallelism between the human individual and the universe. Every person has a beginning in the womb and progresses through birth to life as we experience it. The soul is not a thing inside the body which survives the dissolution of the body; the soul is formed gradually throughout life in response to life's experiences, good, bad and indifferent. But there is offered to everyone the gift of eternal life from God, God's life, going on into

33

a glorious future beyond death in the resurrection of the body. So with the universe: God will redeem it. It had a beginning and it will not be rejected as waste material in the end. God will make something new out of it. The law of entropy is not final. How or when this will be no one can say, though speculation continues about whether the human race will blow up this earth, or the earth will come to an end by a cataclysm of some kind, or by a process of cooling down beyond the point at which it can sustain life. We simply do not know. We must remain agnostic in this respect. But of this we can be assured, if we will let the scriptures assure us: there is a world beyond this world which God will establish, or in the poetic words of the last book of the Bible (Rev 21.1), 'And I saw a new heaven and a new earth: for the first heaven and the first earth were passed away.' All this promised future is carried by the words of the acclamation as it is made in Rite A of the Eucharist in the Alternative Service Book—

> Christ has died
> Christ is risen
> Christ will come again.

3. *God breaks in*

But what of the present day-to-day life of the Christian here and now? It is true we do not know the day or the hour of the Second Coming of Christ in glorious majesty, and it is idle to speculate about it. Even so, Advent proclaims a stirring *contemporary* message. It is to 'keep awake, then; for you do not know on what day your Lord is to come.'

God in the human experience of life often comes to us as a burglar. He breaks in to our routine suddenly, unexpectedly and without warning, and not infrequently, in the dark. This surprises us. We tend to imagine that *we find him* as a result of our search, perhaps in study, prayer or in some consecrated building. We may, but it is just as likely, perhaps more likely, that he will break into our life unexpectedly, and when it is dark and apparently meaningless.

Here is a man too occupied to trouble himself with religion struck down with an illness he certainly did not want. Alone in a hospital bed with hours and hours and nothing to do but think; then God may break into his consciousness like a burglar, and he had better be ready.

Here is a clergyman busy in his study and there is a knock at the front door disturbing him. He resents the intrusion. More especially

34

when he finds a tramp on his doorstep begging for money with the usual half true, half false story he has heard so often. He shuts the door in his face. Then his small son, watching and listening, says, 'Daddy, why were you so cruel to that poor man, he was hungry?' This was God breaking into the clergyman's preoccupation—'When I was hungry you gave me nothing to eat' (Matthew 25.42), another of our Advent readings.

This is the Advent warning. God often comes when we least expect him, and in a guise with which we have not reckoned. It could be through a friendship, a job offered us which seems to be too wonderful to be true, a surprising way out of some difficulty in which we thought we were trapped for ever. Advent says, 'Keep awake, then; for you do not know on what day your Lord is to come.'

And this is the difference between his coming and that of the burglar. The latter comes to steal, to break up and to destroy, but the Lord never. His coming is always to remake, to re-establish, and to bless with his blessing which alone makes us rich. Be ready therefore to recognize the Lord when he comes.

> Wakened by the solemn warning,
> Let the earth-bound soul arise;
> Christ, her Sun, all ill dispelling,
> Shines upon the morning skies.

> (Tr. E. Caswall)

'Even so, come, Lord Jesus.'

9. The Bible and Providence

For all the ancient scriptures were written for our own instruction, in order that through the encouragement they give us we may maintain our hope with fortitude.

ROMANS 15.4 (NEB)

1. *Two coincidences*

I begin with a story. It is not my story but I tell it partly because I read it a few weeks ago in a stiff theological journal not noted for its

35

simplistic piety. It is about an orphanage in desperate need of money to save it from closure. The nuns had no idea where to turn but being devout women, they prayed about it. While they were praying a wealthy man passed by the orphanage and noticed it for the first time in his life. He had not known it was there. Later that day, skimming through the newspaper his eye lit on an appeal for that same orphanage. It moved him, whereupon he took out his cheque book and made a very substantial donation.

Now my question. The nuns took this as an answer to prayer. Were they right? Or was all this a mere coincidence?

Let me tell you another story, my own this time. When I was appointed to a church in Hampstead during the last war, our organ was in desperate need of £1,400 according to the detailed estimate for its repair. £1,400 was a great deal of money in those days, and especially for our struggling church. So we prayed about it. In a matter of days a letter arrived through my letter box, and when I opened it, there was a cheque for exactly £1,400. 'That', you will say, 'is easy to explain. Someone had been told of your need.' But is it easy? According to the lawyer's letter accompanying the cheque, this exact sum had been left to the church by someone who had died some years previously, and the money had only just become available for distribution.

So my question again. Was this an answer to prayer? Or was it sheer coincidence?

2. The Bible and our experience of providence

Let me come to this Sunday, the second in Advent. It has been generally known as Bible Sunday. Hence the collect 'Blessed Lord, who has caused all holy scriptures to be written for our learning . . .' and hence too my text for today's epistle, 'For all the ancient scriptures were written for our own instruction, in order that through the encouragement they give us we may maintain our hope with fortitude.' But how can we hold to the scriptures when they reflect a culture light years away from the world we experience, with its science, its computer technology and its genetic engineering? How can we stomach a book which tells of God leading the Israelites through the Red Sea? And, in the New Testament, of Christ stilling a storm; of twelve men on the day of Pentecost suddenly speaking in diverse languages; and almost as soon as page one of the New Testament is encountered there is a girl conceiving a child without a male input—we call it the Virgin Birth and commemorate it in ten thousand cribs in three weeks' time? I ask you, what are we to do with this old Bible, or 'ancient scriptures', as my text labels them?

I suggest we may have to dispense with them, wrap them up and post them off to some venerable library where the tiny minority of research students can consult them and see how our forefathers used to think in days prior to our scientific revolution—

unless, unless and unless

something in our own experience, like the two stories I recounted a moment ago, *shakes* us into wondering if there isn't after all something much more complex, much more mysterious about life than our modern scientific approach often conceives; and the Bible offers the clue. It tells of a God who orders this world and cares about people, the theological word for which is providence. The Bible is to be read because it enlightens our experience.

3. *Difficulties about providence*

Now, I do not think anyone has the right to claim to profess a religion at all, least of all the Christian religion, who does not hold to some belief in providence. All such a person has is moralism. Not that I wish to underrate its value, or the nobility of moral standards of living. Would to God we saw more such standards in Britain today; but religious faith is more than moralism. It is more than correct behaviour, it is believing in providence, it is believing in a power other than the terrestrial, it is believing in a God who, as well as being in this world, is also beyond it; and he both orders it and cares for individuals in it, the twin pillars of the idea of providence. Granted it is a faith, granted it is incapable of proof, as were my two stories about apparent answers to prayer; but it is not unreasonable to believe that they were providential coincidences.

I admit there are difficulties. It is all very well to wax lyrical about providence in face of the beauties and wonders of nature—the hills and the valleys coloured by the setting sunlight—but what about the Holocaust? What about Aberfan, what about the floods in Bangladesh drowning a million people and the cross-Channel ferry disaster? What

37

about children born diseased and deformed? What are we to make of providence faced with these events?

I know too that there are mathematicians who, faced with the coincidences, come up with what they call the laws of statistical probability. With the thousands of millions of interactions common to earth's five thousand million inhabitants occurring every day, it would be surprising if there were no coincidences. Yes, but there are no coincidences among the five thousand million *individuals* on the earth. No two are exactly alike anywhere.

To examine these difficulties in one sermon is not possible, but they have to be mentioned if the whole subject of divine providence is not to be dismissed as absurdly simplistic. Of course there are problems but to believe in providence is not unreasonable; indeed to make this leap of faith is to live with more hope and fortitude than is otherwise possible.

4. *The rarity of special providences*

One last thought. We are not to fall into the trap of thinking that because some of our prayers have been miraculously answered we can expect God to respond to all our biddings. I cannot agree with the young man who said that he prayed to God every time he visited London to show him a place to park his car, and the miracle never failed. God is not our ever obliging 'nanny'; but there are occasions when the wonder of answered prayer does take place for our encouragement, so that we can continue to believe in providence.

The blunt fact is we all have to live in the light of a very bare supply of miracles, even of special providences. After all they are not on every page in the Bible. There are whole books in the Bible with no intimation of them at all. What we can know is that we have a caring heavenly Father, and our relationship to him is analogous to our relationship with other persons, especially our nearest and dearest. We do not rely on them for everything. We do not run to them with every problem. We need to be independent, and in this sense self-reliant persons. We have to stand on our own feet, and our religion must be such as to assist us in this sturdiness, a quality of stature which a 'cosy' and simplistic piety will not provide.

In a few minutes we shall come forward to partake of the sacred mysteries in this Solemn Eucharist [in St Paul's Church,

Knightsbridge, London SW1]. It all began with Jesus as host at the Last Supper in the upper room at Jerusalem the night before he was crucified; indeed the meal was an integral part of the redemption accomplished on the Cross. Would you not have expected that on this occasion at least some miracle would have been wrought to guarantee that the arrangement for that meal did not founder? But no, Jesus merely worked out a rational security plan, tipping off a householder to provide a room and a sympathizer to show where it was by carrying a jar of water on his head in the street, and two disciples to obtain the necessary bread and wine, presumably from a shop. There was no miracle. There was only careful forethought at the very focus of Christ's ministry and no miracle!

So in the following of Christ we shall have to stand on our own feet exercising forethought and skill most of the time, not least in our daily work at the office, place of business or home. Times, however, will come when we are at our wits' end. Happy then for us if we can know from our own experience, or from what we have been told, that God is close, and God cares, and that divine providence operates for ordinary people like you and me. Then we can trust God and hope in God even with fortitude.

> For all the ancient scriptures were written for our own instruction, in order that through the encouragement they give us we may maintain our hope with fortitude.

I end with a story. In Khrushchev's Russia contacts between East and West were virtually impossible, but somehow a letter was placed in Michael Bourdeaux's hands at Keston in Kent from a school teacher of Russian origin in Paris, enclosing a document of appeal signed by two women. It pleaded for someone from the outside world to intervene with the Soviet Government to stop the closure of one of Russia's greatest Christian shrines. The trouble was no one knew who these signatories were or if the document was genuine, but Michael Bourdeaux thought he ought to visit Moscow and try to find them. It was like looking for a needle in a haystack. Not long after his arrival however he watched two women trying to peer through a crack in the boards surrounding demolition work on a church. He ventured to speak to them, but they were scared of a foreigner. Eventually they listened and beckoned him to follow them. On and on they trudged way out to the suburbs and then into a tiny room where was assembled a tiny group of Russian Orthodox Christians. Greatly daring, after a while he showed the document. Suddenly there was a silence that could be felt. The two women Michael Bourdeaux had spotted peeping through the boards and who had led him to the room revealed their names. It was they who had written the document and smuggled it out of Russia.

My question again. A mere coincidence or divine providence at work? If the latter, ought we not to take the message of the Bible seriously, not least as epitomized in the provoking words of Christ: 'Do not be anxious, the very hairs of your head are all numbered.'

10. The Forerunner

Are you he who is to come, or shall we look for another?

MATTHEW 11.3 (RSV)

Today in our thinking we descend to a prison, a dungeon. I do not know much about prisons though I have been inside two in London (don't misunderstand me, it was to preach), Wormwood Scrubs and Wandsworth; forbidding places, to say the least, but palaces I shouldn't wonder, compared with the prison I am inviting you to visualize now. This was a dungeon deep down in the foundations of Fort Machaerus by the Dead Sea, the whole area deadening to the human spirit, and the dungeon itself dank and dark, designed to destroy any dwindling hope left in the heart of any prisoner clamped in irons there.

And before I proceed I have to warn you not to block your ears on the supposition that all this has nothing to do with you. For have you never been in a prison of doubt: doubt about the reasonableness of the Christian faith let alone its practicability; doubt about the genuineness of someone who professes to be your friend, even to love you; doubt about your ability to carry through a particular piece of work? If you do not know what I am talking about, then, please, bid me, the preacher, 'Good day'. You and I have little in common. There is nothing I can say that will profit. You see, I know what doubt means.

40

1. *The giant imprisoned*

But if you are still 'lending me your ears' come back to Fort Machaerus, Herod Antipas' palace, down by the Dead Sea. The year is about AD 28. The guards have a giant of a man down in the dungeon there. I do not mean necessarily in physique. I do not know about that, though he must have been exceedingly tough—I mean in courage, spiritual perception and leadership. There always had been 'something about him' even when he was a baby boy. Everyone wondered what would become of him. Perhaps a priest with a devoted following in Jerusalem, after all his pedigree was impeccable. But he never became a 'man of the cloth'. Indeed he threw aside normal clothing altogether, normal food and lodging, going to live in the desert, clad only in a rough coat of camel hair with a leather belt to keep it on, and feeding on locusts and wild honey—a scarecrow of a man.

Yet he did not scare people away. That was the marvel. Instead they streamed out to him in droves to listen to his preaching. Not for three, four, five centuries had the land heard preaching like this, not since the old prophets died. Clearly this man knew God, and God spoke through this man. And wonder of wonders, the crowds hung upon his words, every kind and class of person hung upon his words. And more remarkable still they cleaned up their lives in line with what he preached.

And then Herod Antipas got him, got him because Herodias his queen made him get him. She did so because he had the temerity to protest about her marriage to Herod Antipas, being already the wife of his brother Philip. She shed no tears to see him trundled down those steep stairs to the dungeon below Machaerus. When a woman turns to cruelty—and it is rare—her bitterness knows no bounds. She would not be satisfied with less than his life. She waited her chance to pounce, and when it came she saw to it that his head did roll, down there in the dungeon.

2. *The giant's doubts. Our doubts*

I asked you a moment ago if you had ever doubted; this man did, yes, this giant doubted and he was the forerunner of Christ himself, John the Baptist so-called, who had even baptized Christ in the river

Jordan. He came to the point, down in that dungeon at Fort Machaerus, before that woman Herodias took off his head, he came to the point of doubting whether Jesus of Nazareth, whom he had actually baptized, really was the Christ after all. Poor John sank as low as that; the dungeon itself could not bring him lower, his faith had all but gone.

Are you going to blame him? But have you never questioned whether or not the claims we make for Christ can stand up in the modern world? Cheerfully we sing:

> Jesus shall reign where'er the sun
> Does his successive journeys run;
> His kingdom stretch from shore to shore,
> Till moons shall wax and wane no more.

> (I. Watts)

But does his kingdom appear as if it will prevail today? Christian congregations in the affluent West are declining steadily, and in our inner cities the number of people worshipping on Sundays is infinitesimal. What we have seen in our time is the onward march of atheistic Communism, secularism, and the enthronement of science. And has Christianity, even where it has taken a hold, in Africa for instance, brought peace? Today men and women look for political solutions to the problems of society, not religious ones; and even personal problems are carried to the psychiatrist's consulting room, not to the parish priest's vestry. Human reason, it is confidently asserted, will conquer all our troubles given time, even AIDS, even cancer, even leukaemia. They will succumb before the progress of medical expertise as diphtheria has done, tuberculosis and smallpox. And over against the giant worries of our nuclear age does Jesus of Nazareth even look like the Saviour? Does not that role only fit some giant of a man or woman, who shall arise in the future, perhaps a scientist, a politician and a soldier all in one? Who is going to blame the twentieth-century person, looking at the Christ the Church proclaims, for repeating the disillusioned, doubting question of John the Baptist in Fort Machaerus—'Are you he who is to come [that is, the Messiah], or shall we look for another?'

I see from the story of John doubting in the dungeon of Machaerus as recorded in St Matthew, Chapter 11 that Jesus did not blame him. John was worn down; cold, hunger and claustrophobia had worn

42

down the spirit of that fresh air man accustomed to desert spaces. Jesus did not blame him any more than he blames us when, sick in body and mind, we simply cannot find the words to pray. What is more, John felt Jesus had let him down personally. He had preached a triumphant Messiah to come who would act in power and judgement, instead of which he only heard of a man in Galilee healing the sick and evangelizing the poor. The Government was left intact and Roman soldiers still stood on guard at every vantage point. In short, Jesus had made him, John, look silly. Because of all that, and more, doubts, crippling doubts, enveloped John's soul; even so,—please listen to this—Jesus did not blame him.

3. *Genuine doubt. False doubt*

From all this I believe, I cannot help believing, that God views us with compassion, and not with anger, when he sees us beaten down in the despair and disillusionment of doubt about the future of Christianity. Part of the reason, I suggest, is that this kind of doubt is genuine doubt, strange as that phrase may at first sound. Doubt can be a sham and I shall come to that in a minute. Meantime let me say that academic doubt is also a proper disposition in its place, indeed it is essential to the unbiased spirit of enquiry. If no question marks are ever placed, even against what is traditionally accepted, progress towards assurances will never be made. Belief that follows doubt is much more secure than belief which has been too lazy to doubt, or too frightened or too immature.

Doubt can be genuine but there is a form of doubt for which I am confident God has no compassion, for it is a sham, and a pose; I refer to the man or woman who professes to doubt the Christian faith because doubt seems to indicate a certain intellectual or personal superiority. Christian believers, they insinuate, are the simpletons, ready to believe anything. Agnostics on the other hand are the thinkers of the world, the intelligentsia, the ones who give the lead. From this class of doubter come the 'debunkers' of our time, some of them earning large sums of money from the books they write and the television programmes they feed. These people languish in no dungeons of doubt and despair, rather they are up on the battlements proclaiming their wares, causing humble believers to lose the little faith by which they struggle to live in a harsh world. About these,

Christ, as reported in the Gospels, had such hard words to say that I hesitate to repeat them.

I come back to the genuine doubters, and the man or woman languishing in a dungeon of doubt and depression. Is it hard to believe that God has compassion for all such? Some time ago I heard of some students browsing around the theological section of one of the great libraries in Edinburgh. What caught their attention was a bent old man peering closely through his spectacles at one whole row of volumes, fingering them gently and muttering to himself with tears in his voice—'Oh, if only I could believe now as I did when I wrote all these.' As those students watched this famous theological professor, they felt deeply sorry that he had come to this desperate state of painful disillusionment. Is it hard to believe then that God has compassion for genuine and despairing doubt?

4. *The word for doubters*

All the same Jesus had a word for John. It was to bid him to reflect again on what he knew Jesus to be doing in Galilee and Judaea. This is always the word for the genuine doubter whose doubt is painful. Keep your eye on Christ, even if he puzzles you, and you cannot 'take' all the doctrines that are attached to his name. Grasp what you can. Hold on where you are able. Call yourself a Christian even if you would hate to be publicly examined as to the content of your belief, so meagre is it. I should hope you could at least say, 'Jesus is Lord'. Above all we must be honest in God's presence. Honest doubt is better than dishonest belief, though best of all is honest belief. Belief it still is, yet it is belief that moves mountains. Christ said so, and some of us have seen it happen.

11. God Limited and Unlimited

He who has seen me has seen the Father.

JOHN 14.9 (RSV)

I suppose most of us treasure somewhere in our minds what we would call unforgettable sights. One of mine is the leaning tower of Pisa. Of

44

course I had seen pictures of it, who hasn't? But when I first saw it with my own eyes one sparkling Spring day, pitched there on the greenest of green grass as yet unscorched by the fierce Italian sun, the stonework resplendent in its whiteness, the sight all but took my breath away. No amount of descriptive matter in books, pamphlets or lectures could function as a substitute for the actual sight of that fantastic building.

1. *The visible and touchable life of God*

In some such way as this, multiplied a million times, Christianity is unique. No, not because it proclaims distinctive teaching on how we ought to live, though it does that; nor because it sets a standard of morality which makes for our ultimate welfare, though it does that; nor even because it opens up a prospect of personal existence beyond death, though it does that too. Christianity is unique because it declares that God became incarnate in our world and walked about in it so that men and women like ourselves could actually see him and even touch him, thus perceiving what God is like—an astonishing assertion, but one my text from St John 14.9, claiming to be the words of Jesus, makes: 'He who has seen me has seen the Father.'

Maybe we take this 'lying down'. We've heard it before. The text even rolls off our tongue; and as for words like 'Incarnation', they are theological words and so strike no chords within us, or perhaps I ought to say within most of us. But suppose I reverse the sentence. Suppose instead of saying, 'He who has seen me has seen the Father', I say, 'He who has *not* seen me has *not* seen the Father'; heads are jerked up, hackles may even rise. What about the world of nature? Can't we see God there? I have lived the whole of my working life in the sprawling, thrusting, grasping metropolis. Now I live in the country. Am I not more conscious of God than ever before? I think of some of those Spring mornings with the sun not long over the horizon and the air filled with bird song. Can we not see God in the glories of nature? And what about people? What about the acts of sheer goodness where we might least expect them?

A year or more ago I read this story [*Reader's Digest*, December 1987]. During the Vietnamese war some mortar shells fell wrongly on an orphanage killing two children and wounding several more; among them was one eight-year-old girl. She was fast fading through loss of

45

blood. A blood transfusion was urgent to save her life but the blood possessed by the Americans belonged to the wrong blood group; only the injured children had it. So using sign language (for the Americans could not speak Vietnamese), they asked the tiny frightened group of children if any would be willing to help. After a long silence one little hand went up. They lifted him on to a pallet, swabbed his arm with alcohol and inserted the needle into his vein. Every now and again the boy sobbed piteously, but when they asked him if it hurt he shook his head. They were puzzled. Was the operation going wrong? Should they call it off? And then a Vietnamese nurse arrived. Speaking to the boy rapidly in Vietnamese quietened him at once. Now he understood. He had thought he was to give *all his blood* for the little girl so that she would live. And when they asked him why, why he was willing to die for her, he simply replied, 'She's my friend'.

Cannot we see God wherever true love is found? Cannot we see him in religions other than Christianity? Of course we can. God is not confined to any one place, any one experience, not even to religion, and certainly not to any one religion. God has spoken 'in fragmentary and varied form', to quote from the Epistle to the Hebrews, universally and from time immemorial; but once, yes once, something unique happened. There never has been, there never will be anything like it. Listen to the way the writer of the First Epistle of John in the New Testament puts it:

> It was there from the beginning; we have heard it, we have seen it with our own eyes; we looked upon it, and felt it with our own hands; and it is of this we tell. Our theme is the word of life. This life was made visible; we have seen it and bear our witness; we here declare to you the eternal life which dwelt with the Father and was made visible to us. What we have seen and heard we declare to you so that you and we together may share in a common life, that life which we share with the Father and his Son Jesus Christ.

Is it not precisely here that the uniqueness of the Incarnation is to be found? God can indeed be sensed, and in some degree be known, in many and varied experiences and places; but once, yes once, God was able to be seen with ordinary human eyes and even touched with ordinary human hands; that once was when Jesus of Nazareth walked this earth, the Son of God the Father, the One we call the Christ. So

46

my text taken from St John's Gospel presents as his words, 'He who has seen me has seen the Father.'

2. *God limited by his creation*

What do we see? There are many things to see. I wish to point on this occasion to one only. In the Incarnate Son of God we see how God has chosen to be limited by the creation of which he is the architect and constant sustainer.

Let me bring this home. Was Jesus able to be indifferent to the conditions of the environment in which he lived? Was he not rather conditioned by it? Could his mother, for instance, disregard his proper feeding times as a baby because he was the Son of God? Could Jesus, the man of Galilee, be neglectful of the weather and stride forth in mid-winter for open-air preaching? Was he not restricted by the climate of the place where he lived as we are all restricted? And did he not have to obey the demands of sufficient sleep, food and exercise to stay healthy? Had he not to wear the appropriate clothes in winter and in summer?

And you smile pityingly as if I am conjuring up mock questions. But am I? This was the Son of God in Galilee and Judaea who says 'He who has seen me has seen the Father'. Is *God* then limited? Is *God* conditioned by the created order of which he is the architect and sustainer? If so, does this not mean that when God created the world (I cannot avoid risking temporal terms here), in the very act of setting something over against himself with properties of its own, he was actually limiting himself? So it would seem. And so would be the implication of the Incarnation of God. What then comes of our notion of an omnipotent God, a God who can initiate anything and finalize anything and work his will regardless?

All these awkward questions are dragged out of the realm of the theoretical as soon as I mention Aberfan, the Bangladesh floods or the famine in Ethiopia. Could not God, if he be God, have caused the mountain of wet sludge from the coal pits in South Wales to start flowing upwards instead of downwards as soon as it was evident that it would bury a whole schoolful of innocent children? Could not God divert the monsoon rains away from the crowded dwellings in the Ganges Delta? Could not God stop volcanoes pouring out

47

molten lava, so as to render them harmless? The answer to all these questions in the light of my text about the Incarnate Son of God—'He who has seen me has seen the Father'—is 'No'. God is limited by the world he has made.

Is this hard to accept? But look, here is a sculptor—a genius of a sculptor if you like—Michelangelo. Before him is a block of marble. It is not 'any old block of marble', he has chosen it with consummate care, probably visiting the quarries himself at Carrara. He knows that for all his technical skill, he can only make what that block of marble allows him to make. It possesses in itself a certain texture, a certain grain, a distinctive malleability. He has to work within the limits which the marble allows, not least of size. Similarly a painter is restricted by the size of his canvas and what is able to be framed. All this can be summed up by saying that the artist, for all the freedom of original creativeness, is nevertheless conditioned by the medium with which he has freely chosen to work.

So is God. He has chosen to bring into being a world, indeed a universe wherein free human beings shall be able to live; and the planet called Earth, with its most extraordinary and delicate balance of chemical constituents able to support life. It has properties of its own. It must have; which being the case God must to that extent be limited by his creation. The Incarnation therefore is a true picture of God as we know him. He who has seen Jesus has seen God. It is the only such picture in all the world. It shows many things and one of them is how God is limited by his creation.

3. The Incarnation is not the total picture

The Incarnation is not, however, the final, and therefore the total picture of God the Father. He who humbled himself—Jesus our Lord—'taking the form of a servant, and being made in the likeness of men: and being found in fashion as a man, humbled himself to become obedient unto death, even the death of the cross'. He was and is 'highly exalted and given the name above every name'. The Incarnation, I repeat, is not the total picture of Christ, nor therefore of God. There is resurrection and there is exalting. All of which means that it was a proper shudder we experienced a moment ago when we were forced to face the stunning fact of God as limited by his creation. How can God be God if he is not sovereign over all?

The scripture replies, *He will be sovereign over all*. There will come a time when God will be all in all, when there will be a new heaven and a new earth and when there will be no more Aberfans, Bangladesh floods or Ethiopian famines—a time when God's *will will be done*.

That time is not yet, but there are pointers to it in the incarnate life of Jesus in Galilee and Judaea as recorded in the Gospels. There are the miracles, more properly designated 'signs' as in St John's Gospel. Every one of these wonderful works was wrought, you will note, for the removal of what limitations there were in the lives of men and women, be it fever, paralysis, haemorrhage, blindness, deafness—Christ in his ministry was *not limited* in any of those impedimentary situations, nor even by storms, lack of provisions or a death-bed scene; restoration to normality was his accomplishment, whatever the obstacles. Weigh these 'signs' or miracles critically if you must (and you must) but do not delete them 'lock, stock and barrel' because if you do, you will end up with a picture of God totally and for ever limited by his own creation, in which case he cannot be the Sovereign Lord.

'He who has seen me has seen the Father' in his limitation, yes, but he who has seen these signs, those pointers we call miracles accomplished in the incarnate life, has seen also a true picture of God as he must one day be—God all in all.

I have preached you a theological sermon. You may not have followed all the argument. Never mind if only you remember this—there is nothing to compare in all the world with the story of Jesus. Treasure it for all you are worth, for there you will see what God is like as nowhere else, and the sight will steady you in a rough world.

12. The Helpless Christ

And she brought forth her firstborn son, and wrapped him in swaddling clothes, and laid him in a manger.

ST LUKE 2.7 (AV)

I wonder why it was that when St Mark came to write his Gospel of Jesus Christ the Son of God (as he calls him in the very first line), he

49

included no mention whatsoever of the nativity of Jesus? Instead Jesus strides straight on to the public stage as the strong Son of Man, and before you know where you are there he is preaching, calling men to follow him, healing sick people, exorcizing demons—the vitality and energy of the man is amazing. He never seems to stop except for prayer, and even that is activity-orientated. And so the story continues till the bitter end, and what a bitter end it is as St Mark sets it down! Why this portrait? Did St Mark, or St Peter behind him, suppose that the Romans as the addressees of the Gospel could not reckon with a helpless Christ? The Romans never did reckon with helplessness. Their way was to hit life and hit it again, and to hit back when it hit them.

1. *Hard question*

But St Luke's Gospel makes a different start. It tells of Mary who 'brought forth her firstborn son, and wrapped him in swaddling clothes, and laid him in a manger'. It portrays the Son of God as completely helpless. No life is more dependent than the newly born, and we are lured by St Luke's compelling picture of the child Jesus in the manger at Bethlehem to gaze mystified at just that. God incarnate (if the Catholic creeds are to be believed), the God who made the world, lying back in the straw of his makeshift cradle utterly and completely dependent on the ministrations of a young woman for food, clothing and hygiene. What are we to make of this?

I read somewhere in one of the late Bishop Stephen Neill's writings of some babies bereft of their mothers at birth and rescued by a Mission Hospital. This was in India. No attention to these infants could have been more careful, more clinical. Imagine the bewilderment therefore when the whole batch (was it six?) died, and not one from illness, disease or malnutrition. The conclusion was ultimately forced on the nursing staff that the babies had gradually wilted and died because they had never been dandled.

I ask you, did the Son of God live because his mother dandled him? Was he as helpless as that? The suggestion seems outrageous. Can God in any form, at any time, in any set of circumstances ever be helpless? Can he be dependent on *human* support? Can God be dependent on man?

And then I turn to St Matthew's Gospel, and there I read of Joseph stealing out under cover of darkness, taking with him Mary and her child Jesus, making for the road down to Egypt. He was saving the child who before he was born was designated to Joseph as the Saviour of us all. Don't ask me about the historicity of this event. I know something more bewildering—that the safety of the Saviour should depend upon the resourcefulness of a carpenter become an escapee.

And someone wants to cry out, yes, but all this helplessness of Christ belonged to his infancy, it was only temporary, it would not be otherwise if he were God-made-man, as we believe. But was it, do you think, only a feature of his infancy? Does the helplessness of Christ belong only to the cradle? Turn to the closing of his story in any of the three Synoptic Gospels and you will read how he was mocked on the Cross for his helplessness. 'If you are the Son of God', cried his accusers, 'save yourself and come down from the Cross.' But he couldn't come down because he was nailed to the wood. For all the world to see he was the helpless Christ.

I do not know what you make of all this, but you must agree, the story of Jesus is not flat. It provokes with questions like spikes from beginning to end, yes, even from the cradle. When we peep into the manger and watch his mother dandle him upon her knee, we wonder if helplessness can in any way be a feature of the God who made and sustains the universe.

2. *Simplicity justified*

Don't listen to me, the preacher, any more if you can't abide these questions; don't listen to me if you have no wish for the simplicity of the Christmas crib to be complicated with puzzles which jeopardize its childlike appeal. But, you see, I accept your protest. I accept it because I do not wish to obliterate the sentimentality of Christmas myself. I believe it to be essential. I believe God wills it. Why? Because God in his infinite loving kindness and understanding of human nature knows that the vast majority of people are touched by the helplessness of a tiny baby. They warm to a child as to no other. They are not afraid of a child, nor afraid of his strength, nor afraid of his superior intelligence, for he has neither. So God appeared in Bethlehem as a helpless child so that *the good in us* would draw us into his presence. And we are saved from ourselves by being there.

This is the Gospel, this is the good news of the manger scenes, and

Mary the little mother dandling her little baby on her knee. The extraordinary truth is that we are drawn into salvation by the helpless Christ; but then God's truth is extraordinary. It is very deep and very puzzling, but also shockingly simple. Don't lose the simplicity because of the puzzle. Don't lose the depth because of the simplicity. But above all else come to Christ's cradle as you are. You will be welcome. Love the child, and you are loving your Saviour whether you know it or not. And this loving has eternal consequences.

3. *The nature of love*

I have said hard things in this sermon and I have said simple things. I want to state now why I believe the helpless Christ is a true revelation of the nature of God. There is helplessness in God when it comes to dealing with people *because God is love* and love is helpless.

Two years ago I turned again to reread the works of George Eliot, possibly the greatest novelist in the English language. If you have not read them, you do not know what you have missed for a subtle penetration of human nature. In the book entitled *Adam Bede*, there is a gripping story of an attraction between a man and a girl. This is not friendship; in friendship the partners face the same way, both caught by a common interest. No, this is *eros*, this is love; here the partners face each other and are caught by each other. Adam Bede, a fine upstanding young carpenter with good prospects, is caught by Hetty Sorrel, a dairy maid, and she by him—but at no depth. That is the trouble. She has no depth. She is pretty but she is flighty. Attracted by Adam she is also attracted by three or four others, but especially the squire's son, who of course would never marry a dairy maid. But she dreams of him because he smiles at her. She day-dreams of riding one day in a carriage wearing large earrings and Nottingham lace around her collar. None of these rivals are a patch on Adam Bede whose love for her, though maybe blind, is strong, honourable, and lasting. Reading through this novel of some six hundred pages one is left standing amazed at the endurance of Adam's love for Hetty and the lengths to which he is willing to go even after she has been seduced by the squire's son and has even murdered the baby which was the embarrassing outcome. But Adam never wins Hetty. At the end of the day he has to face the hard truth that he is totally unable to make her respond. Love, for all its intensity and even self-sacrificing capacity, is utterly helpless over against the will of the loved one. Love cannot force a corresponding love. It either comes or it does not come.

So it is with God in dealing with people. There is a complicating element of helplessness. Let God stoop as low as may be. Let him assume human flesh as a helpless baby in a pathetic makeshift cradle, let him be nailed in the fullness of his attractive manhood to a torture stake outside a city wall with his jealous foes baying like wolves for his blood, and all for our sake, and out of love for humanity; but he cannot force a corresponding love. We are all free to reject. There is, I repeat, helplessness in God because God is love.

And so over this Christmas period as we gaze reflectively at our representations of a stable in Bethlehem some two thousand years ago, stimulated to see in imagination Mary with her first-born son, wrapping him in swaddling clothes and laying him in a manger, there comes over us the thought of this awful human responsibility—we can reject all this, for what we are looking at in the helpless Christ is a representation of the helplessness at the very heart of God. So the key is in our hands, this is the awe-inspiring thought. And St Matthew and St Luke add three pictures to their nativity story to show us how different people turned their key. There was King Herod. You know what he did. There were the Wise men. You know what they did. There were the shepherds in the fields. You know what they did. What will you do with the helpless Christ? What a question for Christmas!

13. The Holy Family

Is not this the carpenter, the son of Mary, the brother of James and Joseph and Judas and Simon? And are not his sisters here with us?

MARK 6.3 (NEB)

1. *A home and family*

I am going to ask you to imagine something difficult, but I would like you to try. Here are nine people in a room together. The room is small, rather like a whitewashed cube, and it has no windows, only a

53

door for entry. It has a flat roof, or almost flat, just enough tilt for the water to run off when it rains. This is in fact a house, a home. The nine people here are all lying on the floor on mats, with a piece of wood, or a stone, for a headrest. Some have covered themselves with a cloak, for it is winter, otherwise they might sleep on the roof outside. This is the bedroom, kitchen and living room, all in one, with a small space partitioned off for an animal. The furniture consists of one large and commodious chest where the sleeping mats are kept during the day.

And now we shall need to work our imagination even harder. The woman on the floor wakes and looks over the eight other recumbent shapes, not yet stirring. Her husband lies next to her. Close by, close to keep warm, are five boys, and beyond them two girls. She thinks about each one as a mother would, her eyes scanning their slight forms. How different they all are from each other, but none a puzzle except that one over there, the eldest. But then everything about him was strange, it always had been, even from birth. No, she couldn't explain it, but her husband knew, and kept it to himself as she did. And what a husband he was! She thinks of this as she looks down upon him tenderly.

This is a happy family as will soon be evident when they are all 'up and doing'. There is energy, fun and laughter. Then the first of the two daily meals is eaten out in the open where they all live most of the time. The husband is occupied all day as a carpenter, and the eldest boy learns his trade as soon as he is old enough, and strong enough, to work the tools. The girls help their mother grind the daily ration of corn between two heavy millstones on the ground, also outside. They also prepare vegetables for the evening meal. Meat they never see. So day after day, week in week out, year in year out, the routine continues, until tragedy strikes the family. One night there are only eight sleeping figures on the floor. They find it hard to sleep. The father has died, and within a matter of hours been buried. And now the eldest of the boys, turned twelve, is considered a man. So it falls to him to take over the carpentry business to support his mother and provide for the family.

And you think I am describing a slum dwelling in some crowded city, or a barren hut in some desolate refugee camp with scarcely the necessities for bare existence; but what I have been asking you to imagine is the Holy Family in Nazareth in their home—Mary the mother gazing tenderly at her husband Joseph on the floor beside her, and six children, four boys named James, Joseph, Judas and Simon and two girls; and that boy over there, a little older than the others, strong and intelligent, but somehow different. What would become of him? His name is Jesus.

2. *Hard questions*

And now of course hard questions come bubbling up. And doubts begin to arise. And the intellectuals who can find no room for faith alongside their intellectualism offer rationalist answers to the puzzles, for puzzles there certainly are. And the faith of some is damaged, and the faith of others is strengthened, and some have no wish for their picture of the Holy Family to be tampered with, and so shut their ears to every sound of questioning.

But was Jesus really born of a virgin? All sorts of strange genetic experiments are conducted these days but so far no child has been produced without male insemination. So must we reject what Matthew and Luke tell us in their Gospels? Or can we assert, as do some theologians, that what they have provided in their Gospels is their *faith* in Jesus as the Incarnate Son of God, and have cast it in story or picture form, but it did not actually happen that way? Thus, with some such rationalistic approach, the historicity of the Virgin Birth may be denied but the Incarnation be affirmed, and with this in mind the words of the Creed may be recited 'born of the Virgin Mary'. Nevertheless, if no Virgin Birth, all seven of the children, and not only six, sleeping on the floor in the home at Nazareth were born of Mary *and Joseph*.

Suppose however it be maintained that Joseph really was the father of the six only and not of all seven, that is, excluding Jesus—and this has been the consistent faith of the Church down the ages—who was the mother of the other six? Did Joseph and Mary come together, after Jesus was born of the Virgin Mary, and have them? To many this will seem straightforward. There are, however, churchmen who hold a belief in the *perpetual* virginity of Mary and suggest, although there is no scriptural backing for the idea, that they were Joseph's children by a former marriage. This would make Jesus not the eldest but the youngest in the family home who took charge.

And now it can properly be asked, is it *possible* to know the answers

55

to these questions? Can we even investigate? If Jesus' was a virginal conception would Mary broadcast so intimate a fact? And who would believe her? Who believes her now? A child conceived before marriage would be as readily explained in the first century as in the twentieth century. But Matthew in his Gospel wrote 'before their marriage she found she was with child by the Holy Spirit'; and Luke wrote of Mary, 'the Holy Spirit will come upon you, and the power of the Most High will overshadow you; and for that reason the holy child to be born will be called "Son of God" '. No, Paul did not include a doctrine of the virginal conception of Jesus in his preaching in the Graeco-Roman world, but would he in a cultural context where stories of the miraculous births of the pagan gods were common? Could it be perhaps that his travelling companion, Luke, visited Mary in her later years, perhaps while Paul was in prison at Caesarea, and she divulged the true facts to him, for he was not only a sympathetic believer, but a cultured man and a doctor?

We simply do not know beyond what Matthew and Luke have written. How can we know? So maybe it is wise to adopt an attitude of reverent agnosticism to these hard questions, and I emphasize *reverent*. Here we stand on the borderland of the Divine and the human. We had better be careful. How can we produce dogmatic answers in this uncharted territory? Each one of us must make up his own mind and take his own stand. For myself, having agonized over the puzzles, I think it best to lie down with the Catholic Church's traditional attitude of faith and repeat 'I believe in God and in Jesus Christ his only Son our Lord, born of the Virgin Mary', though the puzzles remain.

3. *The break-up of the family*

We come back to that one-roomed house in Nazareth and to the Holy Family complete for at least twelve years until Joseph died, as we presume, for all mention of him slips out of the Gospel narrative after the account of Jesus at the age of twelve accompanying both Joseph and Mary to Jerusalem in Luke Chapter 2. Mary became a widow. Did the burden of the carpentry business and the financial support of the Holy Family then fall on Jesus? And did this early thrust into responsibility produce in him an early maturity and sense of care and compassion? Did it produce a deep sensitivity to his lonely mother and an understanding of women which never left him? And since he was responsible for a family, even though not a parent, did he learn quickly to 'read' people as a parent has to 'read' children? John Chapter 2 v. 24 says 'He knew what was in man'. I think the answer is 'Yes' to all these questions.

What all this means is that the house from which Jesus came partly made him what he was. This is true for every one of us. Good people come from good homes, which does not mean wealthy homes, and bad people come from bad homes, which does not mean poverty-stricken homes. Of course there are exceptions, some glorious exceptions, but the general truth is incontrovertible. Today in Britain we agonize over the violence, vandalism and aggression in our society, the simple root cause of which is certainly not a scarcity of money. There is money about but there is a scarcity of holy families, that is, wholesome families, families in which there is laughter, fun, 'leg-pulling' and some knocking about; but also a sense of right and wrong, caring and, above all, security. The root trouble in contemporary society is broken homes; children growing up uncertain as to which home they really belong as they alternate between the houses of the divorced parents, each with different standards; and homes outwardly stable but full of bickering, strife and tension. And there are the 'latchkey' children.

Homes and families make people what they are. Sometimes when I help with the weekly shopping at the supermarket I overhear—no one can help overhearing—some parent reproving a naughty child. He or she is bawled at, if not sworn at, and physically shaken. And this in the affluent South East! In such cases is there any need to enquire further where some children learn their aggression, their violent temper and their bad language? Surely the crying need today is for the establishment of holy families, that is, wholesome families, families where Christ is honoured. We shall never get Britain right till we get the home right.

Of course the day dawns when the young have to leave home. Jesus had to stay in his home longer than he must have wished. He was thirty before he left. What patience he must have learned! But one evening he laid down his carpenter's tools for the last time and next day made for the Jordan river to begin his public ministry by which we know him. Did Mary weep at his departure? She was no mother I understand if she did not.

Some months ago I came across a little piece in the *Reader's Digest* which I found moving. It was written by the mother of an eighteen-year-old boy about the time when she and her husband saw him off to university. The father shook hands, the mother kissed him lightly on the cheek, and the boy simply said 'Good-bye'. All his thoughts were on the new life ahead. When the mother reached home she cried, especially as her eye caught a photograph of their two sons when they were little boys and turned to their parents for everything. Now the end of all that had come. The family as it was had gone. Both her sons were at university. Yes, she would see them again. Yes, she would be proud of their success, for good-looking and intelligent as they were they were bound to succeed, and they did; but the very success widened the gap. She used to wonder how hard it would be if her boys turned out to be failures. She never thought how hard it would be if they turned out to be successes. But life is like that. And homes and families are like that. They have to break up. If ever the young need an understanding of the parents, especially the mother, this is the time.

I cannot help thinking that Jesus understood his mother when he left home. She did try to interfere once in his public ministry and he was obliged to check her, but he never forsook her. With his dying breath he provided a home for her. Parents must not interfere with their families when the time comes for them to leave home. They must let them go as God lets us all go. He does not interfere. This is hard, but it is right, and the Holy Family to which Jesus belonged was no exception to it. There is an element of bitter-sweet in all loving relationships, not least family relationships, but even this can contribute to our maturity as it did with Jesus.

* * * *

I come back to that one-roomed house in Nazareth and to the Holy Family which lived there. It was a good home because it had good parents even though it lacked almost every facility we should reckon essential. But it had the one thing needful. We shall never know wholesome community life unless we have more holy, more wholesome, families today, homes with this one thing needful, good parents.

14. Christ the Teacher

The people were astounded at his teaching, . . .

MARK 1.22 (NEB)

I wonder if you can remember any of your school teachers, what they looked like, what their names were? I can, and I find my wife can. But then women generally observe people more carefully than do men. But we all, for the most part, remember something about our teachers; some we liked (and for them of course we did good work), and some we didn't like, not to express our attitude more strongly. But never mind for the moment about that dandruff perhaps on their coat collar or those thick woolly stockings, do you remember anything any one of your teachers *said*? Have any of their comments stuck in your mind? Do you recall any of the actual words they used in their teaching? The same, of course, must be asked of sermons. How many sermons can *you* recall?

So here is my question for today—how is it that the actual words, phrases and illustrations from the teaching of Jesus have come down to us? Did someone take Jesus down in shorthand when he spoke? It seems unlikely. Was there anyone around with a tape recorder or cassette? You know the answer. And Jesus never wrote a single book. We are told of him writing on one single occasion only and that was on sand on the ground which he could rub out with his foot. How then has his teaching been preserved, not only in content but also in form?

1. *An impressive teacher*

The first answer has to be because the teacher himself was extraordinarily impressive. He was in the prime of life and those eyes of his, and the way he looked at people, noted in the Gospels, arrested attention from the start. And that voice of his, so strong and clear that he could address a crowd of more than five thousand people in the open air without a public address system, and lower it to speak gently to a woman sitting alone at his feet. The variety of Jesus' addresses was astonishing. He could be compassionate to the unfortunate but biting to the self-righteous. Jesus was never dull. From the moment he began to open his mouth his hearers were either nodding their approval or wagging their heads in dissent. No one could fall asleep.

Time and time again he would prod with a question. What do you think? What is your opinion? What action do you take? No one was in any doubt as to who was the teacher, there was authority even in his repartee with the crowd and how sharp that was! And yet there was no trace of dogmatism, no hint of laying down the law. My guess is that people said 'My! You've got to give it to him! What a speaker! What did you say? He used to be a carpenter in Nazareth? Don't we know the family?' If all this is not true about Jesus as a teacher, how came it that the people hung upon his words (as we are told in Luke 19.48) and that from the very beginning of his public ministry the people were astounded at his teaching (Mark 1.22)?

2. *An impressive form of teaching*

A second answer to my question, 'How is it that the teaching of Jesus has come down to us?' must be that its *form* was memorable. To begin with it was clear, direct and unfudged, and all lit up with illustrations from the contemporary, even homely scene—a farmer sowing seed, a woman baking bread, bridesmaids attending a wedding. Jesus' teaching wasn't 'bookish'. There were no long quotations from ecclesiastical authorities, enough to cause any hearer to 'switch off'. People knew what he was aiming at, and the fact that they understood him left them gasping with astonishment.

And then the *phrases* he used were memorable. You caught yourself saying them to yourself on the way home. 'Can the blind lead the blind, shall they not both fall in the ditch?' 'It is easier for a camel to pass through the eye of a needle than for a rich man to enter the Kingdom of God.' What is more, in the original language in which he spoke—was it Aramaic?—much of what he said was in poetic form with rhythm, metre and that distinctive Hebrew style called parallelism:

'He causeth his sun to rise on the evil and on the good',
and then the balancing phrase to follow,
'And maketh his rain to fall on the just and the unjust.'

It rolls off the tongue. You can't forget it. And the hearers with their largely non-literary education had extra-retentive minds for there were no books. So Jesus took trouble with the *form* of his teaching.

There was no shoddy language. It didn't come 'off the cuff' except in dialogue and argument, and there too he was a master. Altogether Jesus' teaching had style, making full use of hyperbole, simile and metaphor. Indeed the parables for which his teaching is particularly noted are really extended metaphors. And often what he said, he said in exactly the same words over and over again till it stuck in the hearers' minds like the refrain of a 'pop song' in our modern world.

3. *An impressive teaching content*

And then thirdly, there was the *content* of the teaching. The hearers must have cupped their hands over their ears. Was he really saying this? Was he really advocating that?—'Love your enemies, do good to those who hate you.' What? To international terrorists for instance? 'When a man hits you on the cheek, offer him the other too; when a man takes your coat, let him have your shirt as well'—how welcome for the burglars! 'Give to everyone who asks you; when a man takes what is yours do not demand it back.' A welcome then to all twisters and scroungers? Are you surprised to read in St Mark's Gospel that the people were astonished at his teaching if this is the kind of thing he said? And of course they remembered it. Who wouldn't? No clichés, no innocuous platitudes, no 'sob stuff'.

Truth to tell, the content of Jesus' teaching was not only forthright, it was tough. Who for instance wants to hear what he said about divorce? Does the Church today, let alone the general public? And 'enter in by the narrow gate, for wide is the gate and broad is the way that leads to destruction'. I am afraid a good deal of nonsense is talked about the compassion of Christ. Of course he was compassionate not only with the sufferer but also with the sinner, but the woman taken in adultery and forgiven was told 'to sin no more'. There was, there is, a tough streak in Christ's compassion as there is in the love of God. Never for one moment in his teaching did Jesus let it be thought that God is a sentimental old grandfather whom, with a little subtlety, we can easily bamboozle.

4. *The Saviour*

Very well then, the people listened to Jesus' teaching because he was impressive as a man, and the form of his teaching was impressive and

61

so was its content, but can we listen to it today? Wasn't it all rather idealistic and impractical? Did it perhaps fit more easily into the world of his time than into the twentieth century? Or to employ the modern jargon, was not Jesus culturally conditioned so that his words no longer apply? To which I feel bound to answer—the difference between people in the first century whom Jesus addressed and people today is greatly exaggerated. Cruelty and laxity were widespread *then*. A Jewish husband could divorce his wife simply by writing a statement that would easily fit on a postcard—no lawcourt, no expenditure.

No, what we have to grasp is that Christ is the *embodiment* of his teaching. He, and he alone, is what he teaches. He, and he alone, does what he advocates. He, and he alone, lives exactly according to the tenor of his words. Perhaps the main thrust of his teaching can be summed up in his own phrase 'the Kingdom of God'. This is what he came to proclaim, and to teach, but we do not have to go looking here and there for it—in this social programme or that—he, Christ, is the Kingdom of God actually being lived on this earth. He is its embodiment, its incarnation.

Do we fall short of the teaching of Christ? Of course we fall short. We may even fall foul of it; it stings, and we do not like being stung. So we dub it irrelevant in the twentieth century. But, you see, Christ is not simply our teacher from whom we must learn. He is also our Saviour. He stands for us, the righteous, the unrighteous and the half-righteous. He is in fact our Saviour before he is our Teacher. First of all we receive what he gives. We do it without arguing or even talking. All of which will be symbolized or sacramentalized in a few minutes in our Eucharist [at Godstone Parish Church, Surrey]. We simply receive into our mouths the broken bread and the outpoured wine which become for us through faith his body and his blood, and do not say a single word except perhaps 'Amen' or 'Thank you' in our hearts, the Greek word for which is *Eucharist*.

15. Christ the Healer

. . . the power of the Lord was with him to heal.

LUKE 5.17 (RSV)

During the Middle Ages, leprosy was a disease liable to be caught in England. Not that there were large numbers of lepers, but there were some, and of course they had to be isolated from the community. And since this precaution meant their inability to join in public worship, the monks of Westminster Abbey, for instance, built them a little hospital with a chapel attached on a site near what is now known as Hyde Park Corner. Gradually leprosy died out in England and the little leper hospital fell into disuse, but the chapel remained. It became a place of worship for the people who lived round about, until to accommodate them all it had to be enlarged and enlarged again. Finally, about 1900, it was rebuilt on a different site in Prince Consort Road, South Kensington, but Westminster Abbey continued to appoint the Vicar. This was how I came to fulfil a ministry there for nearly twenty years.

I recount this little piece of London history as an illustration of how the care of the sick, even for those suffering from leprosy, was a natural part of the Church's ministry in so far as it followed faithfully in the footsteps of Christ its founder. 'The power of the Lord was with him to heal.' Not that the Church has always been faithful. There grew up in the Middle Ages, for instance, what has been called 'the cult of dirt'. To go unwashed, irritated by coarse clothing, infected with vermin, lacerated with self-inflicted beatings, not to mention the excesses such as living in caves, in the fields like animals, or on top of a pillar like Simeon Stylites for forty years—all this was thought to minister to sanctity and to be an indication of it, but the cult certainly fostered disease. No, wherever the Church has faithfully and intelligently followed the Lord it has been in the forefront of the activity to heal the sick and ease pain.

1. *The situation of Christ's healing ministry*

Let us look for a few minutes at Christ's healing ministry. We are unlikely to grasp its impact unless we are aware of the environment in

63

which he lived. The injured, the broken, the diseased, the blind, the deaf, and the mentally deranged were everywhere. They could not escape notice. Lunatics leered and loped along in public, they were not removed into asylums; the blind felt their way at everyone's mercy, bumping now into this obstacle and falling now into that ditch; and was someone injured in an accident? there was no ambulance to render assistance. Life was harsh in the ancient world and medicine was primitive. No doubt some compassion did exist but the sheer size of the problem drained it away. Moreover, according to the current Jewish doctrine, sickness was due to sin and was therefore culpable; or else an opening to a devil or demon had been provided by misconduct and therefore was not to be pitied. And in pagan communities, most sickness was reckoned to be attributable to fate or witchcraft, and therefore nothing could be done about it. Altogether there was little room for compassion in the world in which Jesus lived and even less for hope.

And then he appeared, giving sight to a blind man here and hearing to a deaf man there, curing a woman with a haemorrhage and a boy of epilepsy. A paralytic took up his bed and walked away cured and a raving lunatic whom no chains could hold down sat still and quiet, talking rationally. All these cases of healing took place just as Jesus happened to encounter them. They were random cures; there was no healing mission as such. The Gospels in the New Testament relate seventeen healing stories and five summaries covering very many more. Clearly only a selection of the cases are provided, sufficient to indicate not only the extent of his healing work but also its range. Once grasp the hopelessness of the outlook for the sick in Jesus' day and we shall not be surprised to learn that when the word went round of what he was doing, the blind hobbled in from every quarter, and fathers and mothers carried their sick on couches that they might receive the touch of his healing hand or come within earshot of his commanding and liberating voice. There never was such a shuffling and crawling and groping and gasping as on the roads and lanes that led to Galilee. Listen to this—

> Jesus went away to the lake-side with his disciples. Great numbers from Galilee, Judaea and Jerusalem, Idumaea and Transjordan, and the neighbourhood of Tyre and Sidon, heard what he was doing and came to see him. So he told his disciples to have a boat

ready for him, to save him from being crushed by the crowd. For he cured so many that sick people of all kinds came crowding in upon him to touch him. The unclean spirits too, when they saw him, would fall at his feet and cry aloud, 'You are the Son of God'; but he insisted that they should not make him known. (Mark 3.7–12).

And what astonished the people was that Jesus never recoiled from the sight of sickness, malformation or disease. He allowed people to touch him, he even grasped a leper eaten up with the disease, he talked to the lunatics and defended the maimed and broken who intruded into synagogues and rich men's houses to meet him. What is more, never once did he say that an illness was the will of God, and though he often said a sick person's cure at his hands was due to that person's faith, he did not refuse to heal because no evidence of faith was forthcoming; he performed the cure out of sheer compassion and nothing else.

I bid you, please, examine the healing ministry of Christ carefully and the environment in which it took place, before you take for granted what happened because you have heard it all before. There is more to this than can be gained by superficial attention. And don't be so old-fashioned in your thinking as to rub out the miracles of Jesus (as we call them) without more ado. If you have the story of Jesus at all you must have healings.

2. *The healings as signs*

Now in St John's Gospel, Christ's works of healing are called signs. We ought to note this. A signpost does not draw attention to itself as an end point but to something else. So the healing works of Christ are not to be read as the completed purpose of his ministry. He never set out to conduct a healing campaign but rather to announce the presence of the kingdom of God. St Mark (at Chapter 1 vv. 14 and 15) is explicit. 'After John had been arrested, Jesus came into Galilee proclaiming the Gospel of God: "The time has come; the kingdom of God is upon you; repent, and believe the Gospel." ' In the course of that preaching (or proclaiming) mission he encountered sick people, and *he turned aside* (please note) to heal them with the result that healings acted as signs to the truth of his message. The kingdom of

God had come because he, Christ, had come, for he is the embodiment of that kingdom. Where he is the kingdom of God is.

To what, then, do the healings by Christ point? There are three answers. First, that the kingdom of God in the person of Christ, the Messiah, has come. This is the good news, this is the Gospel, we should believe this.

Secondly, that the fulfilment of the kingdom of God is not yet present, and we cannot make it be present, be our scientific, political and ecclesiastical strivings never so laudable. But in God's good time it will come, and then there will be no more sickness, no more disease, no more pain, no more crying, no more death, for as the last book of the Bible, the Revelation, puts it, 'the former things are passed away' (21.4).

Thirdly, the healing works of Christ are signs telling how Christians should act whenever they encounter suffering. We should not 'pass by on the other side', not even if the sufferer is responsible for his suffering, like those thousands of people, men and women, hospitalized through smoking-related illnesses, alcohol abuse and those now brought to our attention who have contracted sexual diseases. We are to show compassion. We are to do what we can.

3. *The Church's healing ministry*

There is one aspect of this whole subject I have not touched upon (and 'touching' is all that can be done in a sermon), but which has received considerable attention in the Church of late. Is the Church to continue Christ's ministry of healing? The answer is 'Yes' if we remember that we cannot organize it for we cannot command it. The healings—and *there are healings* through the laying on of hands with prayer and faith—will always be random, because God is the healer. He has the control. But healings I repeat there will be—like those astonishing answers to prayer that sometimes 'leave us standing'—for *our encouragement.* They act as signs for us to persevere in trusting everything to God. We are in his hands, and safe in his hands.

Furthermore there are gifts of healing in the Church, by which I mean that some men and women, not all, have had imparted to them the gift of healing. It is not a supernatural gift, it is a natural one but it becomes a *charisma* belonging to their personality through the operation of the Holy Spirit, who is of course the Spirit of Christ, the

66

healer. This healing ministry is explained by St Paul in his letter to the Corinthian Church (1 Cor 12). We need to remember that it is a spiritual ministry, not a scientific nor a mechanical one. It is Christ's, not ours, though the Church is entrusted with it, but, we must not forget, the exercise and retention of it calls for humility.

4. *The profession of healing the sick*

None of what we have been saying underrates or bypasses the work of the medical profession. With vastly increased knowledge and skill, doctors continue the healing work of Christ whether they be conscious of doing so, or not. God works through medical and scientific hands and brains employing their *God-given* skill now. When however the work of healing is undertaken merely as a science there are dangers. The body is not a mere machine. Pascal was right when he said, 'It is more important to know the person who has got the illness than to know the illness the person has got'. A person is a psychosomatic whole. The lure, however, of what can be done, especially in the realm of embryonic engineering, can stifle the question as to what ought to be done. Dangerously, even the hospital service can become a political football and the purpose of healing be forgotten. Perhaps it is not too much to say that the healing of all sickness is only safe when kept in touch with the Christian insight, for it is a Christian activity. In large measure it stems from Christ the healer, he led the way.

*   *   *   *

I end with a story told by Reginald Hill in his book *The Collaborators* (1987), a little removed from what I have been speaking about but basic to it. It concerns a young French woman during the German occupation of Paris 1940–45. She was tricked into becoming a German secret agent, a collaborator with the Gestapo. When the war was over for France, and Paris was evacuated by the Germans in March 1945, those who had collaborated were rounded up and condemned by hastily convened French courts. The hatred of them was intense and they were forced to suffer every kind of indignity and harshness. Then it was that this young French woman saw her own people inflict precisely the same kind of cruelties that the Germans had inflicted on them. This was the lesson she learned—the hard way.

Cruelty is not the preserve of one nation only. Everywhere the human spirit needs healing, and until this takes place people will be wanting, not to heal pain, but to *inflict* pain. This is the terror of the way in which our world is moving now. Desperately we need Christ the healer. We need to let him heal our souls. And remember this—the power of the Lord is always with him to heal.

16. Christ the Friend of Sinners

After this he went out, and saw a tax-collector, named Levi, sitting at the tax office; and he said to him, 'Follow me.' And he left everything, and rose and followed him.

LUKE 5.27, 28 (RSV)

I am sure he did. I am sure Levi, the tax-collector, did leave everything, rise and follow Jesus at his command. It would be foolish to question the historicity of the event. After all it is reported in the first three of the four Gospels. But a terrible strain is placed on our credulity to believe that there were no antecedents to this sudden renunciation on the part of Levi; tax-collectors are not that rash. But what were the antecedents? I don't know for sure. No one knows. So there is nothing for it but to use our imagination, not wild imagination, but informed imagination. This then is how I picture what happened. I offer it to you for what it is worth.

1. *Levi the man*

Levi was always there, that 'dirty little blood-sucker', as people called him, was always there, always before that grubby little office of his on the quayside at Capernaum. Never a ship could tie up at the quayside, never a ship could cast off from the quayside but he was there, poking into everyone's bundle of merchandise, questioning, arguing, threatening; nothing was to cross that lake from Herod's territory on the other side, or be imported from Herod's territory to this side but that he would impose a tax on it for Herod's coffers—plus what he could slap on top as a commission for his own pocket. Levi's little office by the landing stage at Capernaum was the *douane* and he was the *douanier*, in which capacity he knew all the tricks of the trade. And people hated him for it, everyone hated him. Levi had sold out to the enemy occupying their country. You have to appreciate how the French reacted to their countrymen who collaborated with the Germans during World War II to understand Levi. He was a collaborator with the Roman occupying force, and with their toady, King Herod Antipas. The synagogue had excommunicated him for it, and all his like, and their families as well. They were cut off from the nation of Israel. They were the scum of the earth and made to feel they were. And of course they reacted accordingly. Suppressing what fine feelings they possessed they took pleasure in asserting their authority. Poor people struggling to make a living, women with no one to stand up for them, and of course those well-to-do who might be seeking to hide their wealth—anyone who turned up at the *douane*, Levi was on to them like a bird of prey, out to grab what he could by fair means or foul, usually foul. Levi stank in the nostrils of the community, not least because he made 'a good thing' out of being a collaborator. Not for him a tiny one-roomed house down near the lake like most people, but a fine place up on the hill with a fine view and plenty of space for big parties with his own ilk, whom everyone else shunned 'like the plague'.

2. *Levi recognized*

Now my question, how did *Jesus* react to this man? How would you react? How would I react? There was no chance of dodging Levi, he was always there, sitting outside his little office planted on purpose at the centre of the community's life. Did Jesus bid him 'Good morning', using the customary Hebrew greeting *Shalom*, or did he pass him by as if he were dirt? I doubt if I shall be far wrong, judging by the way the story goes, in suggesting that he greeted him with *Shalom*, not once, not twice, but time and time again till Levi began to expect to be noticed. I will make a further guess—that Jesus himself had entered that grubby little office to pay some due for himself or for his mother who also lived in Capernaum. Let me make a really bold guess—no, I got it from Alexander Whyte's book on the New Testament personalities—some day when Jesus saw Levi harshly exacting a due from some poor widow woman, he intervened, remonstrating with him for his brutality and paying the due himself.

Yes, Levi knew Jesus well enough, and not only by sight. In fact, truth to tell, Jesus disturbed Levi terribly; he wasn't sitting comfortably any more at the *douane*, he was becoming all 'churned up' inside, his conscience beginning to operate, because Jesus was kind to him. No one was kind to Levi.

3. *Levi disturbed*

And then Levi was puzzled. Boat-load after boat-load of ordinary people began turning up at the quayside in Capernaum. They had no merchandise on board, or none worth speaking of, but more often than not some sick person they were supporting, perhaps a cripple, or a case of blindness or even a lunatic. At first they arrived in ones and twos but later on in droves. And they all made their awkward way to where Jesus was preaching down on the lake shore. There grew to be a great crowd. It was impossible to get near, but still the people streamed through Capernaum all making for the lake, all bent on hearing this preacher. He was the man who, unlike everyone else, greeted him every morning—*Shalom!* Levi could not sit still. Normally he had no use for preachers because they had no use for him, they would not even allow him inside their synagogues; not that he wanted to any longer, but curiosity got the better of him. So, disguising himself I shouldn't wonder, he sloped off to stand at the back of the tense crowd. He would see all right. The preacher really *was* the man who didn't spit and pass him by at the *douane*. And he could hear all right. Nothing about the synagogue! Nothing about the Law! But everything about God who both loves people and wants them to love him in return and also to love their neighbours. Poor Levi. He felt wretched. Traipsing back to his little stool outside his little office at the *douane*, he couldn't concentrate on his figures. Day after day this discomfort continued, perhaps week after week, I don't know. Levi's conscience hurt. It hurt terribly. He felt he couldn't endure his job another day. He couldn't squeeze, he couldn't skinflint another customer, he was loathing being a blood-sucker.

4. *Levi summoned*

And then it happened. The preacher had finished for today, the crowds were drifting home and there was the preacher making straight for the *douane*. Right up to Levi sitting on his stool outside his office he went, and stood there gazing at him (yes, he did—read Luke's account in the Greek). There was something about those eyes which got people. They got Levi. He couldn't hold out. Levi knew he couldn't hold out. Jesus knew it too. He'd seen him at the back of the crowd when he was preaching. He could see his face. Jesus could read faces. Perhaps it was working. Faces do work when the heart is deeply moved. And so when Jesus stood before Levi at the *douane*, both knew Levi's time had come. 'Follow me', he said, still looking at him, and Levi did just that, 'he left all, rose up and followed him'—so reads Luke 5.28 (RSV).

5. *Levi's response*

There was a sequel. Levi threw a party up at his house in honour of this preacher who had changed his life and given him peace. But who could the guests be? No one would cross the threshold of one they called a dirty collaborator, no one except fellow tax-collectors, fellow scrim-shanks, twisters and 'wide boys', indeed the riff-raff of the town. They came all right. Anything for a party. And the drink wasn't lemonade. And there was Levi the host, and there sat Jesus next to him as the honoured guest. And when the party got going and everyone was enjoying themselves, there appeared faces at the open doors, Pharisees, Scribes, infuriated by what they saw. They lost no time in voicing their complaints, not to Jesus but to his disciples—'Why do you eat and drink (note 'and drink') with tax-gatherers and sinners?' (Luke 5.30). He himself knew what they were saying, and on another occasion (Luke 7.34) even repeated their charge to the crowds assembled to listen to him. ' "Behold", they say, "a glutton and a drunkard, a friend of tax-gatherers and sinners." '

6. *The preaching involved*

So now we know. Jesus did not ask his hearers to be respectable before he could sit down with them. He did not require them to abandon their scurrilous ways before he would acknowledge them. He saw Levi at the *douane* when everyone else tried not to see him because they hated him. This is what is meant by the phrase, 'Christ the friend of sinners'. He does not, however, count sin of no consequence. When

Levi accepted the friendship of Jesus he abandoned the trickery of his trade for evermore. But this was the difference between Jesus and every other preacher of the time: he showed how God loves every one of us, whatever we have done or omitted to do, long before we ever thought of loving him. This is why the crowds flocked down to the lake at Capernaum when he was preaching; they had never heard anything like it, and it was not even necessary to enter a synagogue to hear it!

Why do the first three Gospels all make a point of including this call of Levi in their narrative? Surely because they knew Jesus had used this startling event as a public demonstration of what his Gospel was all about—the forgiveness of God for men and women, be they never so sinful, if they are willing to receive it as a gift. Don't forget everyone knew Levi, he was always there, down by the quayside, at the *douane*; and now he was no longer there, instead he was following Christ. What was more, Christ had chosen him. The people of Capernaum never ceased to wag their heads in astonishment. Levi accepted! Levi, that decadent little *douanier*! Then, of course, there must be a chance for everyone. Nobody need feel left out of the love of God. And that, precisely, is what the Gospel of Jesus Christ is all about, or, as St Paul put it very plainly, 'God shows his love for us in that while we were yet sinners Christ died for us'. (Romans 5.8)

17. The Victory of the Cross

Do you suppose that I cannot appeal to my Father, who would at once send to my aid more than twelve legions of angels?

MATTHEW 26.53 (NEB)

Jesus was in a tight corner when (according to St Matthew), he asked this rhetorical question of his disciple whom St John identifies as Peter. It did not arise from an academic seminar or a devotional retreat, it burst out hot from a scuffle after dark between determined men armed with swords and cudgels, and at their head, Judas, the traitor; the whole place—the garden of Gethsemane—lit up with the flames of smoky torches. Peter blazed with fury to discern the face of a fellow disciple leading that mob creeping forward to strike. Very well, he would strike too! Not for him to betray. 'No, he would defend his Master.' And before anyone, even Jesus, could check his movements, he whipped out the sword he had hidden under his cloak, half expecting trouble, and lunged out at the head of the High Priest's servant, who fortunately ducked. It was above this shouting, this uproar, that someone heard what Jesus said to Peter: 'Put up your sword . . . Do you suppose that I cannot appeal to my Father, who would at once send to my aid more than twelve legions of angels? But how then could the scriptures be fulfilled, which say that this must be?'

What do you see here? Do you see a poor trapped Jesus, darting his eyes this way and that like some frightened and overpowered animal, desperate for some way of escape? Do you see a defeated man, a victim of injustice, a body about to be broken on the wheel of Rome's imperious cruelty? Yes, the handcuffs were ready, the lawyers were busy trumping up their charges, carpenters were knocking up that crude wooden gibbet in some out-of-the-way backyard; indeed the whole stage was being set for the Cross of Christ; but I ask you, is this all you see? Christ as *the victim*? Then what are you going to do with that rhetorical question wrung from the lips of Jesus and addressed to Peter amid the scuffle in the garden: 'Do you suppose that I cannot appeal to my Father, who would at once send to my aid more than twelve legions of angels?' I think you will have to revise your view of the crucifixion and see Christ, not simply as the victim, but also and pre-eminently Christ as *the victor*. It is this interpretation of the Cross I would like to commend.

1. *The Cross an abomination*

First, then, let me say this, the Cross was an abomination, too low down to be labelled beastly—even animals behave better than men crucifying men; no, the Cross is devilish, but it happened, it is historical. Christ was strung up like that, too repulsive to be contemplated realistically; the Gospels draw a veil over it, and even painters, for the most part, have stopped short within theological interpretations instead. And what is so awful is 'the fact (to quote Herbert Butterfield) that Jesus Christ was not merely murdered by hooligans in a country road; he was condemned by everything that was most respectable in that day, everything that pretended to be most righteous—the religious leaders of the time, the authority of the Roman government and even democracy itself which shouted to save Barabbas rather than Christ.' So not only was the torture of the Cross appallingly repulsive, so also was the public gloating over it. I repeat, the Cross was an abomination. It was not the will of God.

Let us pause here for a moment. Surely we cannot think God wanted this to be done to his beloved Son? What sense could there be in talking about God as the loving heavenly Father—and rather glibly these days I fear—if this was his plan for Jesus? What ordinary father among us would ever conceive of this idea? What is more, I am convinced that God does not will any suffering of any kind on any one of us—cancer, arthritis, epilepsy, yes, and AIDS—God does not *inflict* pain, he does not *punish* with disease, these things are contrary to God's intention. And the application must be made to Christ and his Cross. It was an abomination to God, and I myself can find no relief whatsoever in the theology that some have advocated, that God looks for sacrifice in life, and wanting an example of perfect sacrifice, sacrifice to the uttermost, selected his beloved Son for it. I find this repulsive. No, the Cross of Christ was not the will of God the Father, it was the will of the men who did it and gloated over the performance that first Good Friday.

2. *God's identification with suffering*

But now a second point and a most important one. When Jesus saw the hostile mob burst into the garden, led by Judas coming up to betray him with a kiss, and the swords, the cudgels and doubtless the ropes and handcuffs, and knew what at last was about to happen, he did not side-step the horror, nor even appeal for divine protection. He said to Peter, 'Do you suppose that I cannot appeal to my Father, who would at once send to my aid twelve legions of angels?' But he made no such appeal; 'Lord save me'. This was the prayer he did not pray. He gave himself up to his captors.

Why was this? It was because he wished to identify personally with the pain and misery that has been the lot of the greater part of humanity since the world began. You do not believe this sorry estimate of the human story? Then you should read the Gifford Lectures of the years 1935–37, given in Glasgow by Professor

W. Macneile Dixon, where you will find it carefully substantiated.

I know of course that it is in the face of this that the case for atheism finds its strongest support. Why has God made a world like this? Is it possible to believe in a God at all in the face of it? And there would be nothing to say if Christ had pleaded for those twelve legions of angels, and so opted out of the world as it is. But he did not ask for protection. He went forward to meet his torturers, accepting the worst they could do without complaint or any appeal to human rights.

I am not suggesting that all difficulties are hereby solved. Much hard thinking is still necessary to believe in a God who made a world like this, but the observable fact is that the Cross of Christ has enabled millions of people to bear their lot in life and to continue to believe in God.

Ernst Wilm, a German pastor, has told of his experience in the summer of 1942. With about four hundred prisoners, he was being marched to a farm outside the concentration camp to work. Every time they passed by a wayside crucifix the Catholics among them, both German and Polish, doffed their caps. This was unheard of in the presence of the S.S., but strange to say no sentry objected. And Ernst Wilm, Evangelical though he was, also doffed his cap. The sight of the crucified Christ in a world of hunger and deprivation, rejection and cruelty made them feel they were not forgotten. Christ was present even in Dachau.

This is what Christ wished us to know. This is why he did not ask for those twelve legions of angels. God is with us wherever we are. Not even the ghastly aspects of the world's story cancel God out. We are not left with an impersonal fate. There is a Gospel *because of the* Cross not in spite of it. And no other religion has as its central symbol a pain-drenched figure down in the drains of human existence. But he triumphed there. Therein lies our hope.

3. *Christ the Victor*

And now this. Jesus *chose* the horror of the Cross deliberately. This is what he wanted. This is what he intended. I bid you grasp this point. A man is not defeated if he obtains what he wants. In spite of outward appearances he is the victor of his situation, and not its victim.

How was Christ victor? He was victor because he drained the actions of his enemies of every vestige of value from their point of view. They thought that getting him crucified they would get him out of people's thoughts for ever, but quite the reverse has happened. It is largely *because of the Cross* that the world still remembers him; indeed it is hard to think of a symbol more widely known and recognized than the Cross. The blunt fact is that his opponents did not put him out of the way by crucifying him: they put him 'in the way'. Truth to tell, their plans were turned upside down, and if they reckoned on Good Friday evening with Jesus dead and buried that they had beaten him for ever, never was a victory more hollow than what they achieved, never a victory more aptly labelled a Pyrrhic victory. In short their victory was their defeat. Christ conquered by the Cross.

And this is what the Cross stands for—the turning of defeats into victory. And Christ achieves it still in the hearts of people. When we are down, deep down, depressed and defeated, and in that condition turn to Christ, the very defeat and the turning are the conditions of our victory. In some mysterious way—and whatever theories of atonement are propounded by the theologians, the mystery remains—the Cross of Christ takes away the barriers that shut us from God. Somehow we are set free and stand on our feet again. Somehow Christ's strength flows into our weakness, changing it. Because he conquered, in union by faith with him, we conquer.

And what is more, it is the influence of the Cross of Christ that has done most for the banishment of all crosses, racks, thumbscrews, torture chambers, whips and rods, indeed every instrument of cruelty which is an abomination to humanity and decency that has disfigured our world. By choosing to suffer the abomination of the Cross, Christ has liberated the urge to outlaw all such abominations.

O yes, Christ really was, really is, the victor. We should thank God from the bottom of our hearts for his Cross and Passion. It has altered the world.

> In the Cross of Christ I glory,
> Towering o'er the wrecks of time;
> All the light of sacred story
> Gathers round its head sublime.

> (Sir John Bowring)

18. The Easter Triumph

Alleluia: for the Lord God omnipotent reigneth.

REVELATION 19.6 (AV)

1. *The cause of despair*

I don't like asking you to picture eleven miserable men. I don't enjoy being miserable myself, and I don't like being made miserable by other people; but I can't help myself as I try to open up the Easter Gospel because it is rooted precisely in that doleful situation. Eleven men weeping and mourning. I am not imagining this; Mark 16 verse 10 says so; and the fact that St Mark may not have written these particular verses where this statement occurs (a textual matter) casts no doubt whatsoever on the incident. Jesus had died. Some, if not all, had actually seen him die. What would you expect but that his followers would be broken men? Perhaps it is as well we can't see them. It is heartbreaking to see men heartbroken. It is hurtful to observe them struggling not to cry, and failing miserably.

And you say to me, 'Why are you labouring their grief? Have not people lost dear ones before and since? Are not bereavements listed in every day's newspapers? And don't they sometimes surge in like a flood? There was the ferry disaster, and the Enniskillen bomb outrage, and the King's Cross Underground fire. And some of us can remember the long and sickening casualty lists of the war-time years. Bereavement is a fact of life, and few people escape it. So why the spotlight on these eleven broken men?' I'll tell you why—because they were convinced that *Jesus could not die.* And I am not surprised. So when it happened, they went down to hell.

Consider for a moment the experiences these men had had with Jesus, what they had seen, what they had heard, and the electric effect it all had on the people in Galilee, Judaea and the countries beyond those borders. His fame heaped up rapidly. In everybody's eyes Jesus was an extraordinary figure. And there must have been miracles. Tempting as it may be to rub them out of his story as incredible, it is like asking for an umbrella without a frame. They are embedded in his ministry and cannot be deleted without distorting the whole. So had these weeping and mourning disciples really been

77

witnesses to the healing of a leper with a word; and a paralytic being made to walk; and a deaf and dumb man speak? Did they actually live through the stilling of a storm on the Galilean lake; did they take round five barley loaves and two small fish to feed five thousand men; did they watch two cases of bringing back to life of young people just dead, and one actually buried four days? I ask the questions. If they did, is it surprising that they were convinced that he who could do such things *could not die*, he was the Prince of life? But he did die; that was the earth-shattering puzzle for them. He died on a cross just like any other common man.

I tell you, it wasn't simply because of bereavement that these eleven men were utterly miserable; it was because nothing seemed to make sense any more. Jesus' powers got him nowhere. Scheming priests and callous soldiers instead got him where they wanted him, and he appeared powerless. The taunt was even voiced as abuse at the foot of the Cross: 'he saved others, himself he cannot save'. So what price faith in God now? What use in trusting God? What point in religion at all, or even goodness? The whole thing is a sham. Nothing makes sense any more. Wickedness has the last laugh and the forces of nature 'red in tooth and claw' are the ultimate controllers of our destiny, there is nothing else. Jesus, the miracle worker, dead in the grave proclaims that terrifying message. No wonder these eleven men were utterly broken, for it was they who had lived closest to the drama.

2. *Rationalizing the defect*

But these eleven miserable men did not stay much longer than forty-eight hours in their slough of despond, though one, Thomas, took a week. Every Christian who knows anything at all about the Christian story is aware of Easter and the transformation it brought. These men were soon up on their feet proclaiming a vibrant life—affirming a Gospel sufficient to set the world wondering. The rise of the Christian Church starts there.

But how were these men stood up on their feet? Was it that, when they thought about what had taken place, they came to see how Jesus was a martyr? He was a martyr for that in which he passionately believed, namely trust in God as the heavenly Father; and, because he was willing to give his life for that belief, he made it priceless, he lifted it so high there can be nothing now too valuable not to be expended to give it pre-eminence. So he was the victor in being the victim. And who shall say there is no truth in this? There is indeed a profound truth here. We can catch a glimpse of the power of martyrdom when we see how careful the law is in apprehending a criminal not to make a martyr of him. But will this do as an explanation of the revivification of the faith in Jesus of these eleven miserable men? Bear in mind that they were for the most part what we loosely call 'working men'. Do such people engage in such subtle philosophic reasoning? Do they engage in it and come to buoyant, mind-reversing conclusions within the space of forty-eight hours? Most of us will find this hard to believe. Then what did happen to cause their transformation?

Let us concede that it must have been some *external* event which jerked them out of their lethargy up into bubbling confidence. But what was it? Was it a vision or series of visions of the Christ they had known? Have not many of us, bereaved of someone we loved, suddenly and momentarily 'seen' them in the street, or in the old familiar setting? But if this 'trick of the mind' seems too slender a foundation for the Easter Gospel, could we assert that the visions of the risen Christ (so called), as recorded in the Gospels, were God-induced hallucinations; that is to say hallucinations specially, indeed miraculously, provided by God so as to provide the world with the Easter message of life beyond death? But will this explanation meet the real need of the beaten down disciples, which was that Jesus could not die? Death could have no power over such as him. But it did have that power apparently. They saw him die.

3. *The ultimate miracle*

So an Easter Gospel operating at the level of mind and spirit will not do. Easter cannot convey the Gospel the Church has traditionally taken it to convey if the miracle of it stops short at the physical body of Jesus in the grave because there can be no interference with the laws of nature, not even by God; they are fixed. Miracle at this level there cannot be. So in the ministry of Jesus the nature miracles (so called)—the walking on the water, the stilling of the storm, the feeding of the five thousand with five loaves and two small fish must be rejected, though the healing miracles may be believed because we see the operation of the mind over the body today in the practice of psychosomatic medicine.

No, the resurrection of Christ on Easter Day, interpreted in terms of vision only, does not meet the case of the eleven bereaved, miserable and disillusioned disciples, even though there are advocates for it who claim that by means of it they can profess belief in the resurrection. Very well. Let it be. Nevertheless problems remain. What happened to the dead body of Jesus when the crucifixion was over? It is not easy to lose a body. Don't we know? And was Jesus so insignificant a person that nobody bothered? Had not the Jewish authorities and the Romans ganged up to do away with him, and that publicly?

But, leaving aside the events of the death and burial of Jesus, let us ask a theological question. What does Easter proclaim? Is it the Lordship of Christ and of God over all that is; or does it proclaim that Lordship *only* in the realm of mind and spirit? Is matter then alien to God's authority and power? Is there a realm completely outside the divine operation, an area of life subject only to the unalterable laws of nature? If so, then undoubtedly the miracle of Christ's resurrection must stop short at his grave; it would not operate there, and the nature miracles attributed to Jesus in his ministry must be rejected. Are we to believe that God's power does not supersede or interfere with nature?

But this is not what the Church has believed. It has accepted that the tomb of Jesus where he was buried stood empty on Easter morning. The physical body had been raised. It had been transformed by the power of God into a spiritual body in which he, Christ, appeared from time to time to those who believed in him. It was this which charged the eleven preachers of the risen Christ. It was this which let them know that they had not been deluded in the wonderful works they saw Jesus perform in Judaea and Galilee. There was no 'jiggery-pokery'. Religion is not a sham. Virtue is worthwhile. Faith will be justified. God's power is over the whole of life and death. Nothing is beyond the reach of his transforming power, not even the grave. This is the Easter message. 'O death where is thy sting? O grave where is thy victory?' 'Alleluia: the Lord God omnipotent reigneth.' He reigns *over all*.

19. The Holy Spirit

'But when the Advocate has come whom I will send you from the Father . . . he will bear witness of me.'

JOHN 15.26 (NEB)

I would like to tell you about a Youth Club. It was part of the activity of an ordinary suburban church and consisted of about twenty or thirty teenagers. It had two or three good leaders in succession though none of them possessed any particular gifts of personality, education or status in the community. The youth met on Saturday evenings, played games, discussed among themselves and finished sometimes with a short prayer and meditation. There was nothing in the way of teaching or direct evangelism, and church attendance was voluntary and unorganized. In the course of one or two years, a week's holiday away together was arranged. This was all. Of the group, however, two became church school teachers; another, the head of a State Teacher Training College and later inspector of theological colleges; another, headmaster of a well-known public school; another, a university professor of ecclesiastical history; two if not three, clergymen; another, the Matron of her own nursing home—to mention only some of them. How is this to be explained? The only answer that will stand up to inspection is that somehow in the Christian fellowship of the club the Christian way of life became a reality for them personally and they went on to develop their own individual potentialities. We might say that their Christianity was caught rather than taught.

1. *God at work*

Today we are thinking about the Holy Spirit, and first of all I would like to say that the Holy Spirit is the One by whom and through whom Christianity *gets caught*. This is not quite how the Bible expresses it, but consistent with its way of speaking by means of pictures and figures of speech rather than abstract theological phrases, it refers to the finger of God and the hand of God. They represent God at work, God touching people, God exercising his power in the world; and this is the Holy Spirit.

One of the most famous of pictures is Michelangelo's 'The Creation of Adam' in the Sistine Chapel at the Vatican. Do you remember it?

81

God depicted as a man reaching out and touching Adam with his finger; that is to say, God at his work of creation, a representation inspired by Genesis Chapter 1 telling of the primitive chaos and the spirit of God brooding on the face of the waters and dry land appearing.

Fingers are fascinating parts of the human body. Who is there who is not astonished at the facility of some great pianist like Rubinstein or Ashkenazy creating the most glorious music by the skill, strength and delicacy of his fingers? Or some great painter—Raphael, Corot, Goya—give them pigment and put a brush in their fingers and look what they can do! And the touch of the fingers or of the hand by one person on another is a means of communicating feeling, concern, even love; and it is inspiring. How significant then that in the Bible, God at work, creating, loving and inspiring, namely the Holy Spirit, is represented by God's fingers and God's hand.

And so we read in Luke 11.20 of Jesus challenging his opponents, 'If it is by the finger of God that I drive out the devils, then be sure the kingdom of God has already come upon you.' And how it had been asked of John the Baptist when only an infant, 'What will this child become? For indeed the hand of the Lord was upon him.' (Luke 1.66) And how when the men of Cyprus and Cyrene began to preach to pagans in Antioch 'the hand of the Lord (translated in the NEB as the power of the Lord) was with them and a great many became believers and turned to the Lord' (Acts 11.21). All this is a way of saying God, that is the Holy Spirit, was at work here, this is how the power of the Gospel catches people. This is how Christianity is caught. So it was in the Youth Club of which I spoke a moment ago.

2. *Making Christ contemporary*

Secondly, the Holy Spirit is he who makes Christ contemporary. If we stop to think for a moment, it really is odd how central a place Christ occupies in the hearts and minds of so many millions of people, and has done for hundreds and hundreds of years. After all we know so little about him. He occupied a public stage for only three years at most, and in what a backwater that stage was set—Galilee and Judaea. We do not know what he looked like, how tall he was, what was the timbre of his voice, nor even with certainty in what language he taught, Aramaic or Greek. He wrote no books, he set up no organization. He was of course a preacher and teacher, and we have records in the Gospels of what he said, perhaps even some of his actual words; but though the teaching was sublime and penetrating, it was no more than could be on the lips of a great Hebrew prophet. And he exercised a ministry of mental and bodily healing, but so have others, even if less startling. What is more he was a man of the first century; his clothes, his life-style and his manners would be strange to us. He would not know how to use a knife and fork. Jesus of Nazareth was in fact 'culturally conditioned', to employ the modern jargon. We are all culturally conditioned, limited by the age and place where we pass our lives. How comes it then that this remote and historical figure occupies so central a place for so many millions of people? How is it that he means so much to us?

> How sweet the name of Jesus sounds
> In a believer's ear!
> It soothes his sorrows, heals his wounds,
> And drives away his fear.

(J. Newton)

How is it that we are gathered in this church today in his name to sing hymns like this? The answer is—the Holy Spirit is he who makes Christ contemporary, or, as we have it from the lips of Jesus himself as John 14.26 asserts, 'But when the Advocate has come, whom I will send you from the Father—the Spirit of truth that issues from the Father—he will bear witness of me.'

So it is a mistake to see Christians as followers of Jesus in the same way as men and women might be of Aristotle, Descartes or Karl Marx. We do not have to know first of all the biography of Jesus or the substance of his teaching, even though it is edifying to know as much as we are able and where we are able. No, a Christian is someone *caught by Christ's spirit*, the Holy Spirit, encountered in the life of some other man or woman, and in the worshipping community we call 'the Church'. And when we have *been caught*, then Jesus of Nazareth steps out of the pages of history, where he is not walled in, and becomes for us the contemporary Christ, the Christ whom we worship and in whose name we pray. It is through the Holy Spirit that we have the Christ of faith, who is not other than the Jesus of history, but that same Jesus risen.

And when did this work of interpreting Jesus begin? At Pentecost,

83

that is Whitsunday, following close on Easter Day, the resurrection day of Jesus. So the Christ we know is the risen Jesus, the Christ of faith; the Holy Spirit makes him contemporary, our contemporary. We can be in communion with him now.

3. Developing our potentialities

And now, thirdly, the Holy Spirit is he who develops our potentialities.

In September 1987, Bishop Lesslie Newbiggin had an article in the *Expository Times* entitled 'Evangelism in the city'. In it he described his work as the minister of a small congregation in a Victorian building situated immediately opposite Winson Green prison, Birmingham. In an area of very high unemployment, and an exceptionally high proportion of single parent families, and a rich ethnic mix in which native Anglo-Saxons form a minority—altogether an area of relative deprivation, it is not surprising that the response to the preaching of the Christian Gospel is small. Nevertheless there is a response; lives are changed and genuine Christian characters do emerge, but there is a problem. These converts quickly develop potentialities and skills, and so their earning capacity. Not surprisingly they soon wish to move out of the depressed area just at the time when they become precisely the sort of people that would benefit the locality. This is to be regretted but we should not miss observing what are the results of the working of the Holy Spirit in the lives of the most ordinary people—gifts, potentialities and skills appear.

Those of us who have worked over a period of years helping to train candidates for the Christian ministry will have seen this for ourselves. I can think of clergymen exercising an effective ministry one of whom began as an office boy, another a lorry driver, another a railway porter, as well as candidates from what is called 'the upper end' of the social scale. Their acquired skills were indeed a mark of the working of the Holy Spirit, but much more their new characters, bringing to mind the words of St Paul in his letter to the Galatians (5.22) '. . . the fruit of the Spirit is love, joy, peace, long-suffering, kindness, goodness, faithfulness, meekness, temperance'; so different from the works of the flesh—fornication, uncleanness, lasciviousness, a list too dismal to continue.

This is the point for us to grasp. Whenever we come into contact with a Christian character, there we may know that the Holy Spirit is at work. He operates especially in the Church, but not only there. The Spirit of God is the source of all good inspiration; in art, in music, in literature and in organization. The Spirit of God broods continually over all God's creation bringing forth new life, new beauties and new benefits. Perhaps inspiration is only safe when its origin is recognized. This is a big subject, too big for this sermon. Here however we can plant our feet on firm ground—the Holy Spirit is he who develops the gifts and potentialities that lie within us all. Surely no call could be more wholesome than the call to respond in faith to Christ, by which means the Spirit is able to do his work, his redeeming, edifying and inspiring work, a benefit to the community beyond compare.

20. Who is Jesus?

What we have seen and heard we declare to you.

1 JOHN 1.3 (NEB)

1. *Three personal experiences*

(a) A few years ago I visited the Holy Land. Our party arrived in Jerusalem after midnight and was housed on the eighteenth floor of an hotel. I awoke next morning at five o'clock, as the day was breaking, and went to the balcony window. And there it was—I shall never forget it—the Holy City perched on a hill, its stout Turkish encircling walls pink in the rising sunlight. Later that morning we walked the streets of this history-soaked place, much of it cruel; and we visited Bethlehem, Hebron, the Dead Sea, Jericho, Galilee, Nazareth and so on. I learnt, as you would expect, more about the background against which Jesus lived out his life nearly two thousand years ago, but it did not bring him any nearer. If anything it took him further away. I saw him as belonging to a way of life more unlike mine than I had imagined and knew that had I by some strange phenomenon encountered him as I turned the corner in a Jerusalem street, I should be unable to understand a single word he uttered, or share with him the way he lived. I am an Englishman of the twentieth century and he a Palestinian Jew of the first century.

(b) But then I treasure another experience. I have described it in

85

my book *Have you anything to declare?* It was the eve of my fourteenth birthday. My father had been dead ten years, the influenza scourge of 1918 saw to that, and my mother was left to bring up her two boys alone. There was no Social Security in those days. My elder brother had left home and I was sitting with my mother at the dining room table. I cannot recall how the subject arose but she, who had been brought up as a Roman Catholic, explained how Jesus had lived and died for me. Crude maybe, but there was no emotion and no fuss. I confessed no sins. Fourteen-year-old boys do not sit still anyway for more than about five minutes, and I was no exception. But I believed what she said. From that day I have understood what the word 'Gospel' means, and my allegiance to Jesus, begun then, is something without which I wouldn't be where I am today.

(c) Let me turn to one other incident before I ask my question. Before I visited Jerusalem I went to stay with the head of what we should call a Theological College in Germany. I had not met him before but I discovered that he and I were born in exactly the same year, but he in München-Gladbach of non-believing parents and I in Sheringham, England. How could two people be more unlike? He became an officer in the German Army during the last war and was taken prisoner on the Russian front where he was kept till 1949. One day in the prisoner-of-war camp a fellow officer produced a Greek Testament from somewhere and they both sat down to read it. Somehow the Jesus they read about seemed a contemporary figure; so contemporary that my friend gave him his allegiance and, after returning home from the prison camp, got ordained, and, like me, became a preacher.

2. *Jesus is known existentially*

How do you explain this? How do you explain a figure who becomes more remote the more you delve into the historical and geographical factors that condition his background, and yet is able to make an impact on a fourteen-year-old boy sufficient to determine the whole course of his life? And to exert the same kind of influence on an unbelieving officer in the German army sufficient to turn him into a prominent theologian? And that boy and that officer, identical in age, but so different in nationality that their countries were on opposite sides in the war? How explain the power of this remote historical figure in the twentieth century? How explain Jesus of Nazareth? Who was he? Who is he?

You will have observed while I have been speaking how frequently I have referred to myself—indeed my introduction has been wholly given over to three personal reminiscences. This has been deliberate. The question, 'Who is Jesus?' can only fully be answered existentially. I have to tell you who Jesus is to me. You have to tell me who Jesus is to you, if you are a believer. The whole Christian Church, the great body of Christians today and down through the centuries, has to tell who Jesus is to them; and putting them together we shall come closer to providing an adequate answer as to who Jesus is. We cannot determine his identity by detached examination. Jesus—like truth, beauty and goodness—is not discoverable by science, but only existentially, only through personal experience.

3. *Jesus known historically*

Now I am not so foolish as to suggest that nothing at all can be known of Jesus from the outside. Jesus is by no means the private preserve of believers, and certainly not of the Church. Jesus does not belong exclusively to vestry or to sanctuary, in spite of the inclination of some ecclesiastics sometimes to domesticate him in this fashion. Jesus stands out on the frontier between the Church and the world, accessible to both. Yes, we can discover something about Jesus' identity from the outside (so to speak). We can deduce that he did actually exist. If the records we have of the Gospels are held to be suspect because they are Church records, we have the allusions to him in the Latin writers Tacitus, Suetonius and Pliny the Younger; and whatever objections Josephus the Jewish historian could heap together to incriminate the Church, he never alleged that its leader had never existed.

But what can we know about him from a critical examination of the Gospels? That he was an intriguing figure, very strong yet attractive if you were willing to surrender to him; otherwise it was possible to hate him even to the death. No one lightly cast in their lot with him, his standards were too high, his assessment of people too penetrating to be comfortable; yet Jesus was a man to whom others instinctively turned, one whose words you listened to and treasured, a man whom it was impossible to visualize except in a position of leadership, and everything due to his personal authority which relied on no external authorization whatsoever.

There have been others before Jesus, and since, who have drawn multitudes after them. What we see going on in Iran today is traceable to Mahomet. There is also Gautama the Buddha. And how many millions are there whose lives have been moulded by Karl Marx? Who then is Jesus? Who then is Jesus if he is in any essential sense different from any other great leader who has drawn half the world after him?

No complete answer, I repeat, is possible on objective, scientific or observable premises alone. We may assess Jesus as a prophet, a teacher, a moral reformer, even a pioneer of social justice. Liberal Jews are ready to account him one of the most outstanding sons of their race; and there is truth in every one of these evaluations; but at the end of the day Jesus does not completely fit any one of these categories; there is always a question mark.

4. *God encountered through Jesus*

If, therefore, we are bound to recognize that the identity of Jesus is not accessible to those who, whatever their sympathies, would not count themselves his followers, who or what is Jesus to committed Christians? Surely the one through whom they encounter God now. This is who he is. It is an experiential or existential assessment. We call him the Christ of experience; and the arresting fact is that he may be known with only an imperfect or sketchy knowledge of the Jesus of history. Probably the great events of Christmas, Good Friday and Easter will ring a bell, a phrase or two from the Sermon on the Mount, perhaps a parable or miracle story, but that is all. The situation is at the farthest remove from embarking on a course of study and, as a consequence, enlisting as a follower or disciple. There are cases of this and the story of my German friend may be one of them. What is more common, so common as to be the norm, is that a new spirit is encountered in a Christian community, a church, like this one [Liverpool Parish Church], or a single individual. A personal response is made to this spirit, it is in fact the Christian spirit, to be more precise it is the Spirit of Christ. So we are introduced to the Christ of experience before we turn to the historical Jesus, and this experience is deepened and strengthened through worship, sacraments, prayer, service of others and by faith committed throughout the ups and downs of life. So Christ is our contemporary whatever the date or place of our circumstances. We know him so we live with him.

This giving of priority to the Christ of experience as I am doing, is a repetition of what actually happened in the early days of the Christian movement. There were no lives of Jesus, no biographies, no written portraits of Jesus for thirty years or more after his death that could be studied. What did exist was the Christian community displaying a new spirit in the Jewish and pagan world. And there was worship and there were the sacraments and there was preaching in which stories of Jesus were told, but above all and through all and in all was the proclamation that God had come in Jesus to die for sins and to rise again, making available newness of life. So the Christian community knew and responded to the Christ of experience all before there existed any accounts that could bring knowledge of the story of Jesus. The Christ of experience, I repeat, comes first.

Who then is Jesus? Who is this historical figure who walked the lanes and streets of Galilean and Judaean towns and was finally crucified by Roman soldiers outside Jerusalem's walls? Who is this Jew of the first century who was brought up in a home no self-respecting Town Council today would begin to reckon as fit for human habitation: a single-storey one-roomed building, virtually without heat, light or sanitation; who knew nothing of the internal combustion engine, electronics or even a push-bike, and who spoke a dialect of Hebrew called Aramaic and that, maybe, with a Galilean accent. Jesus is the Christ of my experience, the Christ of your experience, the Christ of the Church's experience as Lord: 'Jesus is Lord'!

I finish with a story. A Trade Union official, Left in politics, was walking along Margaret Street in London's West End. He was not a Christian and said so, though his wife was. Something made him turn into All Saints' Church, a place quite unfamiliar to him. As it happened the Vicar was there and they came face to face. Pleasantries were passed and they began talking. For reasons that are inexplicable the Trade Union official 'took to' the Vicar and they met again. One day not long after, he came home to his wife as a committed Christian, and proved it by being confirmed. He is still a Christian and has just been made Chairman of an Industrial Mission.

Who is Jesus?

You will never know unless you are willing to take into account stories like the one I have just told you.

21. New Birth

'The wind blows where it wills, and you hear the sound of it, but you do not know whence it comes or whither it goes; so it is with everyone who is born of the spirit.'

JOHN 3.8 (RSV)

Today is Whitsunday, or Pentecost as it is often called. And so I invite you to visualize a man making his way, quite alone, after dark, through a grove of olive trees seeking out a certain garden. He does not edge his way furtively, for he would not know how, but he trusts no one will see him, nor guess his intended destination. He has disguised himself, not heavily but sufficiently to allow him to pass virtually unnoticed should he encounter anyone on the way. For all the disguise however, and all the stealth, a careful observer would note, even by the way he walked, let alone the cut of his clothes, that he was no commoner, but an aristocrat, a wealthy aristocrat; and even more striking, an aristocrat with all the marks about his eyes and ageing face, of being a scholar as well, a man you looked at twice if you met him once.

And now we hurry on ahead to the garden he is seeking. A group of men are seated there in animated conversation. All of a sudden their speech is silenced. What was that? A rustling of leaves in the wind? But no, there is a distinct footfall on the gravel. And then the lone figure appears. He makes straight for the group. There is sufficient light for them to see his face. They are astonished for they recognize him. He is the supreme Rabbi of Israel, the pre-eminent preacher and teacher on whose words the whole nation hung; his name was Nicodemus. And the group startled by this intrusion? Who are they? They are Jesus of Nazareth and his disciples in the garden he often frequented on the slopes of the Mount of Olives outside Jerusalem's walls.

90

I make no apology for dramatizing this encounter of Jesus and Nicodemus taken from St John Chapter 3, because the Bible itself proclaims its message, not in abstract theologies but through human stories about people, and this is true of the basic Pentecostal theme.

1. *Jesus and Nicodemus*

Come back, then, to the garden, back to the encounter. Jesus and Nicodemus facing each other, two men worlds apart. Nicodemus opens up with a diplomatic overture, the kind ecclesiastics employ in ticklish situations. Concessions, if not flattery, constitute the opening gambit. So here, 'Rabbi' . . . Would Jesus fall for that? 'Rabbi', but he held no Rabbinical authorization or training whatsoever. 'Rabbi, we know that you are a teacher come from God! Yes, of course the bulk of the religious authorities reject your ministry, but not quite all, some of us having observed your works cannot resist the conclusion that God must be with you!' But just as Nicodemus was drawing his breath to make a proposition, perhaps about some sort of ecclesiastical merger or consensus in order to avoid a dangerous clash of religions in the city, Jesus cut in, 'Truly, truly I say to you, unless one is born anew he cannot see the kingdom of God.'

That did it! And maybe it 'does it' for us too. We do not like this phrase, 'born anew' or 'born again'. It conjures up images of revivalist preachers, hot gospellers and all the razzmatazz that often goes with it. And ever since Jimmy Carter held office at the White House, the press has splashed about the term 'born again Christian', till it has come to mean a narrow fundamentalist, an embarrassing if not brash type of pietist—and, what is worse, the implication is that no Christian who has not undergone a startling conversion experience ought to be called a Christian at all. What a pity this is! And what a travesty of the truth! The phrase 'born again' only occurs once in the whole New Testament, and even there, in this Nicodemus story, the Greek word could equally well be translated 'born anew'. Furthermore, according to the Gospels the word was never employed by Jesus except in conversation with a theologian, it was not for popular use; and as we shall see, not even Nicodemus could make 'head or tail' of it. So let us clear the decks of our minds of popular misconceptions, so that we can hear what the story of this strange encounter between these two men under the trees in the garden is saying.

2. *New birth by the Spirit*

It is saying that you cannot begin to know the real God if you rely only on the tools of intellectual reasoning and cultural conditioning, be they never so sharp. Of course they have their part to play, indeed to do without them altogether is impossible, but they are like the component parts of a motor car—the engine, the driving shaft, the gears—be they never so finely tuned, the car will still stand there in the garage unless there is electric current to switch on and activate the parts.

Poor Nicodemus! Was there ever a face more pathetically blank? How Rembrandt would have painted it! A face which showed he could not fathom what Jesus was talking about. For him everything had to be rational, everything able to be comprehended by the natural man and his trained faculties. Had he not given his whole life to the furtherance of this discipline? How could this man Jesus, standing there under the trees in the garden half shrouded by the darkness of the night, speak about the limitations of the human to grasp the infinities of the Spirit: 'That which is born of the flesh is flesh and that which is born of the Spirit is spirit. Do not marvel that I said to you, you must be born anew'? And Jesus, watching Nicodemus, was astonished at his ignorance of this basic principle and said so. 'You, the teacher of Israel and you do not know this? O Nicodemus! Nicodemus! You reckon nothing is real unless it can be understood, nothing serviceable unless it can be explained. But listen to the wind, Nicodemus, listen to the wind—you hear the sound of it but you do not know whence it comes or whither it goes. And yet all over the world men will be employing the winds to sail their ships, turn their mills, separate their wheat from the chaff. So it is with everyone who is born of the Spirit.' The spiritual life is beyond rational explanation, all you can do is surrender to its influence, humbly, trustingly and willingly, as if you were beginning life all over again in a kind of new birth. One begins from there or not at all in the spiritual life.

3. *New birth for the Church*

I wonder what happened to Nicodemus after this. Did he trace puzzled steps back through the olive grove to his palace in Jerusalem still hoping nobody would see him? Did he sit up for most of the night turning over in his mind what Jesus had said—'The wind blows where it wills, and you hear the sound of it, but you do not know whence it comes or whither it goes; so it is with everyone who is born of the Spirit.' But how can these things be? Is there not a danger here of opening the floodgates of emotionalism, from which fanaticism is never far distant. Must we not beware of enthusiasm in religion? Look at the harm it has done! But could Nicodemus get Jesus' words out of his mind? Could he get this person out of his consciousness? Apparently not, or else why, months later, did he make that mild protest on Jesus' behalf when his fellow Sanhedrin councillors ganged up to condemn him to death? And why was Nicodemus of all people seen helping Joseph of Arimathaea take down the body of Jesus from the Cross with ointments ready for the burial, if what John tells us in his Gospel, Chapter 19, is true?

And this is what I can't help wondering, though granted I have nothing specific to go on: was Nicodemus still in Jerusalem on the day of Pentecost? And did he come to hear of something taking place for the disciples of Jesus which could only be described symbolically as a sound from heaven like the rush of a mighty wind and filling the house where they were sitting? If so, can you doubt that he went back in mind to that garden and the night under the olive trees when Jesus said 'Listen to the wind, Nicodemus, listen to the wind. The wind blows where it wills, and you hear the sound of it, but you do not know whence it comes or whither it goes; so it is with everyone who is born of the Spirit.' And did Nicodemus know then that what was happening was the birthday of the Christian Church, the birth from above, the new birth? Nicodemus might have thought, and you and I might have thought, that when the disciples had Jesus among them teaching them, this was all that was required. But no, they had to wait till they were born from above, born of the Spirit, the Greek word for which is *pneuma*, exactly the same word as for wind. And nothing else conditioned this birthday taking place; not the disciples' education, nor lack of education; religious culture or lack of religious culture; achievement or lack of achievement. Only one condition was necessary, and these one hundred and twenty men and women (or thereabouts) gathered in Jerusalem fulfilled it—they believed in the risen Christ. So at Pentecost the wind blew, they were filled with the Spirit, they had a birthday with which there is nothing to compare.

4. *New birth for the individual*

And someone says to me, 'This is all very well but nothing like this has ever happened to me. To me religion is a rather pedestrian affair; doing one's duty, avoiding wrong, showing compassion, supporting the Church, contributing to good causes.' But have there never been occasions, rare maybe, when you have suddenly felt a thrill? It could have been a piece of music which all but took your breath away; it could have been an occasion when in someone's presence you suddenly felt time to stand still; it could have been the hundred and first occasion when you knelt to receive the sacrament of Christ's broken body and blood, but this time you said to yourself—as the words were spoken *Christi Leib für dich gegeben* [The body of Christ given for you]—'Was it really? Even for me? For me!' On those occasions you were born anew, born from above, the Spirit of God broke in to you from outside. No, you can't explain it, nor can I. 'The wind blows where it wills, and you hear the sound of it, but you do not know whence it comes or whither it goes; so it is with everyone who is born of the Spirit.'

I hope you won't count this too grand a story but I saw it. I was attending the Archbishop of Canterbury at the Lambeth Conference of bishops in Canterbury Cathedral in 1978. From my place next to the Archbishop seated in the Chair of St Augustine, I looked down on a sea of episcopal faces from all over the world, mostly white, but many brown and some black. I saw them come up to receive the sacrament of the body and blood of Christ in their outstretched hands. That, and the historic setting stretching back hundreds of years was deeply moving, but what 'got me', no other words will do, what got me was the choir singing, and O so softly, that simple negro spiritual—'Were you there when they crucified my Lord?' I had a struggle to hold back my tears; so, I guess, did scores of bishops in that Cathedral. Anyone would have to have been made of stone not to feel the truth of God at that moment.

What will you call this? Inspiration? New birth? The words do not matter. What does matter is the realization that the knowledge of God comes *from God* not from ourselves. It breaks in from outside in different ways and at different times for different people, *throughout life*. 'The wind blows where it wills, and you hear the sound of it, but you do not know whence it comes or whither it goes; so it is with everyone who is born of the Spirit.' Without this new birth we can only know *about God*; with it we can know him as he is. And the experience is open to us all; and especially to those who believe in the crucified and risen Christ.

(This sermon was preached in St Mary's German Lutheran Church in London.)

22. The Eucharist's Historical Root

For I received from the Lord what I also delivered to you that the Lord Jesus on the night when he was betrayed took bread, and when he had given thanks, he broke it and said, 'This is my body which is for you. Do this in remembrance of me.' In the same way also the cup after supper, saying, 'This cup is the new covenant in my blood. Do this, as often as you drink it, in remembrance of me.'

1 CORINTHIANS 11.23–25 (RSV)

Let me speak plainly. I hate and abominate a quarrel. I know some people revel in confrontation. I have been around sufficiently long to have watched people deliberately provoke discord for the sheer fun of seeing 'the sparks fly'. This is not to say I warm to 'tame' people, to men and women who either possess no opinions of their own or are too dull or too lazy to express them. No, I like people who are alive, but not the quarrelsome, and not those who foment tensions in Christian congregations. Quarrelling is particularly out of place there.

But it happens. It has always been happening. We can read about it in the New Testament. The Church in Corinth was a hotbed of dissension partly due to the quarrelsome nature of the Corinthians; and one of the places where it flared up was the Eucharist. Indeed the situation became so disgraceful that St Paul was constrained to write

95

to them about it in a letter. I said just now that I hate confrontations but I have to admit that sometimes good comes out of them. So here at Corinth. Let me tell you what happened.

1. *The Eucharist disgraced in Corinth*

The Church members at Corinth were keen on fellowship. All around them in Greek society were clubs of one kind and another at which eating and drinking played a prominent part. Not surprisingly the Christians in the city, separated from these carousings, expected the Church to provide a fellowship centre for them, and it did; and there was no class distinction, and no financial distinction; they were together because they shared a common faith in Christ. First they met for a kind of supper party, no doubt a cheerful affair, and then they moved on to celebrate the Eucharist, embodying their faith. But the smoothness did not last, quarrels broke out. They had begun with the arrangement that each member brought to the supper what he or she could afford, the poor little, the rich much, and they shared the gifts among all present equally. But after a while the rich felt embarrassed to be eating with the poor, and so kept themselves apart in another room enjoying a splendid feast; and the poor, separated off, deprived now of the gifts of the rich, went hungry. Then all came together for the Eucharist, some overfed and 'over-wined', others deprived. And of course arguing and quarrelling ensued. What would you expect? So St Paul had to write to them about it. You will find his letter in 1 Corinthians Chapter 11, and strong writing it is, telling the Corinthians that because of their behaviour their Eucharist stood, not as their salvation, but as their judgement; they were profaning the body and blood of the Lord.

But good actually came of all this, as I said just now sometimes happens. The disgraceful situation in Corinth made St Paul take up his pen and provide an account of how the Eucharist was initiated in the first place. It is the earliest account of the Last Supper which we possess, antedating what we have in the Gospels. Let me read it to you. It is quite short but full of meaning.

For I received from the Lord what I also delivered to you that the Lord Jesus on the night when he was betrayed took bread, and when he had given thanks [Greek, *eucharistēsas*], he broke it and

96

said, 'This is my body which is for you. Do this in remembrance of me.' In the same way also the cup, after supper, saying, 'This cup is the new covenant in my blood. Do this, as often as you drink it, in remembrance of me.'

2. *The Eucharist rooted in history and revelation*

First, I would have you notice that in order to put the Corinthian Church straight St Paul went back to history, Christian history. And we too can never be sure about what we ought to do if we drift away from this historical and historic foundation. Christianity begins not with a philosophy, nor an ethical code, much less a social or political programme, it starts with what happened. Listen: 'The Lord Jesus on the night when he was betrayed'. What could be more specific? . . . Judas was wrapping his cloak round him and skulking out under cover of darkness to play the part of 'a mole', tipping off Jesus' enemies as to where and how they could arrest him without a public riot. *On that night* Jesus took bread, gave thanks (*eucharistēsas*) broke it and said . . . So it was not 'at any old time' that Jesus instituted the Eucharist, he did it *while he was being betrayed to death*. The Eucharist cannot possibly be separated from the death.

Secondly, please note, that St Paul had delivered to the Church at Corinth what he himself had received. Listen again: 'For I *received* from the Lord what I also delivered to you.' So he considered it his duty to pass on the tradition, thus keeping in touch with what had happened. This historical root must never be blurred, never let go. And note, too, from whom he received the tradition; it was 'from the Lord'. That is to say, he had not merely heard about it, been told about it, or read about it, the Lord had disclosed it to him, which must mean the risen Lord. So the Eucharist is not only rooted in an historical event, it is also a disclosure of the risen Christ. Therefore it is never outdated. It is always contemporary. It makes the death of Christ relevant now. So Jesus, when he had taken the bread, given thanks, and broken it, said, 'This is my body which is given *for you.*'

O the barrels of ink that have been used by pens commenting on the verb 'to be' here. 'This *is* my body.' Is the body of Christ then actually present in the Eucharist? Is there a real presence? Yes, there is; but there is also a real absence, for he went on to say, 'Do this in remembrance of me' which would not be possible if he were still

97

there. All of which is why I follow the Anglican teaching. We do not believe in transubstantiation, that is the transformation of the bread and wine into the actual body and blood of Christ (appearance notwithstanding); nor do we believe in Zwinglianism, that the Eucharist is a mere memorial of what took place on the night Jesus was betrayed. No, Christ is really present but in a spiritual sense to those who come to the Eucharist in faith.

I think perhaps one of the most moving celebrations of the Eucharist of which I have read took place in a garret on the fifth floor of a Parisian mansion in the Rue Notre Dame des Champs in 1794 on Christmas Eve. But of course Christmas had been abolished as had the month of December; it was now called Frimaire for it was the third year of 'Liberty, Equality and Fraternity'. The Countess Lafayette, held a prisoner there, took out from under her skirt a little piece of black bread and a little wine in a mug secreted from the communal dining room downstairs. Then, unpinning from its hiding place beneath her bodice the silver crucifix which her mother had given her, she propped it against the chair-back, the only piece of furniture in the room except the straw palliasse, and placed two stumps of candles on either side, with the tinder box ready. Then she waited. Would he ever come? But he did come, Père Carrichon, disguised as a carpenter come to do a repair, a priest she knew. He laid out a hammer and nails making it look as if the candles were to help him see the work should anyone enter the room. Then he raised his hand in blessing. And as the rhythmic phrases of the ancient Latin liturgy, though whispered, poured into the tiny room, the Countess closed her eyes and sank to her knees, back again in the certainties of the faith by which she had always sustained her life, and which began in the night when the Lord Jesus was betrayed, took bread and broke it, and offered it in the same way. 'This is my body, this is my blood which is given for you. Do this in remembrance of me.' The little room in Paris in 1794 led right back to that historic event, back to Christ himself, the ugly revolution all around notwithstanding.

3. Two warnings

There are, I think, two warnings that we need to heed with reference to our attitude to the Eucharist. We can let it slip into little more than a contentious issue of interpretation, almost fighting and quarrelling over it, and we can cheapen it.

There is of course a debate at the moment about the ordination of women to the priesthood. Ought a woman to be the celebrant? There is a question here which must be faced by both sides in the argument. In having a woman as the celebrant, is the historical link with what happened on the night when Jesus took bread, broke it and said 'Do this in remembrance of me' strengthened or weakened? Jesus was not a woman, he was a man. But, says the other side, the maleness of Jesus is not the fact of importance. Jesus in initiating the Eucharist stands for humanity, male and female. He is a representative figure. This however, is a concept *derived* from the historical Jesus. The *primary* fact is the man Christ Jesus taking the bread and taking the cup. What the Eucharist does, everywhere it is celebrated, is to go back to what happened on the night when Jesus was betrayed.

Doubtless the debate will continue and opposing answers be given. This however must be said; it is wrong to fight over the Eucharist, differ in our views though we may, and it is wrong to use the Eucharist as a platform for protest. Some, alas, have fallen into this trap.

A second danger lies in cheapening the Eucharist. You remember what happened at Corinth which earned St Paul's stern rebuke? The members of the Church there wanted a jolly party. Fair enough. There is a place for jolly parties in Church circles. But in Corinth they let their preferences slide over into the Eucharist and become quarrels. So St Paul brought them back to the night when the Lord Jesus was betrayed. It was an awful occasion, by which I mean an occasion full of awe, terrible awe; nevertheless he gave thanks (*eucharistēsas*), broke bread and distributed it saying, 'This is my body' and placed the *broken bread* in their hands. Could the communicants that night ever forget the solemnity? Was there any hint of mere 'mateyness' taking over? But who shall say there is no danger of this in our parish communions today? We need to be on our guard not to cheapen our contemporary celebrations. Maybe we have come nowhere near turning them into our judgement as the Corinthians apparently did, but we may severely limit them as means of Grace.

This is clear. We must be careful never to drift away from the historic and historical root, that is, the night when the Lord Jesus was betrayed and took bread and broke it. Of course we rejoice. Of course we sing his praises. We cannot be unduly solemn, for the Eucharist is a thanksgiving; but do not forget the price that was paid for it; our salvation was paid for in blood. This is what the Eucharist is all about.

23. The Forgiveness of Sins

For in Christ our release is secured and our sins are forgiven through the shedding of his blood.

EPHESIANS 1.7 (NEB)

1. *A Christian fundamental*

Whenever we come to church for worship, making use of either the Book of Common Prayer or the Alternative Service Book, we encounter reference to the forgiveness of sins. Indeed we encounter more than a reference. In the Apostles' Creed we confess that we actually believe in it, along with such weighty matters as belief in the Holy Spirit, the Holy Catholic Church, the resurrection of the body and the life everlasting. In addition we are bidden in the course of our worship to kneel down and confess our sins, corporate as well as individual, after which a priest solemnly makes a declaration of forgiveness.

We can't profess to be Christians and play down this doctrine of forgiveness of sins. It is a Christian fundamental. But what are we to make of it? Let us be frank. Is modern man really troubled about his sins? Is it not unrealistic to drag in this subject of forgiveness on every occasion of worship? In so far as secularized man thinks about religion at all, and it isn't often, isn't he far more likely to concentrate on doubts rather than on sins? Is there a God at all? Are there absolutes of right and wrong? Is there a meaning in life or does it not operate on a basis of chance, fate or destiny—call it what you will? In the light of these questionings does not fussing over the forgiveness of sins appear futile?

We are not, however, at the moment analysing the attitude of our secularized contemporaries but thinking about the man or woman of

100

sufficient awareness of God to come to church for worship. Our question is, 'Can we, ought we to approach God in either prayer or praise without taking seriously the forgiveness of sins?' Certainly, if God is no more than a man 'writ large' which is what pagan gods are. But suppose God is what the Bible reveals him to be, utterly and unapproachedly beyond us in holiness, wisdom and love; in that case we dare not enter his presence except on bended knee, confessing ourselves sinners and asking his forgiveness. And the more sensitive the man, the more sensitive the woman, the greater the readiness to do this; and conversely the more dense the man, the more dense the woman, the greater the *unwillingness* to do this. Otherwise we would resemble the recipient of a decoration seeing no incongruity in arriving at Buckingham Palace in his gardening boots on the day of the presentation by the Queen.

2. *The penalty of sins*

But what is forgiveness of sins? Is it the remission of the penalty? Is it being let off the punishment for wrong-doing? It certainly is not.

About a year ago I found myself sitting outside a surgeon's consulting room door waiting my turn. After some minutes there was wheeled in beside me, in a chair, an elderly man also waiting his turn. He could not stand. He could not walk. He told me he was completely dependent on his wife's nursing at home. And then for some strange reason he felt compelled to own up. 'It's all my own fault', he said, 'I've been a fool. Couldn't leave the bottle alone. Hard stuff it was mostly, rum and gin. I suppose I've burned my insides out. Sometimes they feel like it.' I said I was sorry, and we talked a bit. I saw that he felt better for his confession, stranger though I was to him, but I also saw that even if he reached the point of divine forgiveness for his sins—and there was no chance in that temporary queue outside the surgeon's door to get round to this—he would not escape the penalty for his sins, he would, most likely, never leave that wheeled chair.

But wait a minute! Yes, it could be that, healed in mind and soul through receiving the forgiveness of God for his sins, and being assured that God had not on account of them cast him off, he could recover a quality of life otherwise totally beyond his reach. For this is what the forgiveness of sins provides at once—the restoration to

101

fellowship with God. The barriers are gone, coming and going is opened up, prayer is possible, peace of mind is possible, and with the healing of the soul new life begins to dawn, even though he might never walk again, though miracles do sometimes happen.

3. *When forgiveness is immoral*

Forgiveness cannot therefore simply be construed as remission of the penalty for sinning. It does not provide a cheap way out of the consequence of wrong-doing. There is nothing cheap about forgiveness. It costs to offer it and it costs to receive it.

I am reminded of a middle-aged couple who offered friendship and hospitality to a younger woman in need. A warm and kindly association continued for years but the younger woman grew bored. She wanted more out of life. She complained of being exploited, and left, banging the door behind her. Advised by her neighbours she half apologized, was forgiven and the old association was repaired. But her pride rankled about that half apology, and a year later she stormed out again. This time there was no apology of any kind. It was not a price for forgiveness and restoration she was prepared to pay. The cost to her pride was too great.

Forgiveness is not cheap to receive, neither is it cheap to give. If it is cheap and easy to give it is immoral. In the autumn of 1987 there was shown on television a play in seven parts by Olivia Manning called *Fortunes of War*. It was about a couple called Guy and Harriet Pringle shifting their residence from Bucharest, to Athens, to Cairo on account of the advancing German army in World War II. The arresting feature of the story was the bewilderment of the wife at the cool, if not cold attachment of her husband to her, faithful though they were to each other and never at cross purposes. One day in Egypt she spent a day with an army officer touring the pyramids, her husband being busy. In the evening she told him where she had been and he, without a twinge of emotion, just as if he were commenting on the weather said, 'Now I suppose you would like an affair for a while'. She had no thought of it, but he would have forgiven her if she had. That is what cut her to the quick. What his forgiveness indicated was that he didn't care tuppence about marital infidelity, and with that the nagging feeling deep down inside her that he did not all that much care about her. When forgiveness is easily given without agony, it is immoral. It means the forgiving person does not take sin seriously.

3. The Cross and forgiveness

And so we come to God's forgiveness. God cannot simply forgive us even though we repent. I said *simply*. Forgiveness is a costly business for God, even for God, no, most certainly for God. Were it not so, the implication would be that he did not care one way or the other whether we sinned or not. A shrug of the shoulders would deal with the matter. Then what would become of the moral law? What would be the consequent deduction about the structure of the universe? Surely that there was no morality in it, rather it was, it is, a-moral. Then nothing matters any more, life is futile, and the end of humanity is in sight.

So if forgiveness is possible at all on the part of God it has to be costly. It also has to be costly if the relationship of God to man is one of love. Whenever there is a loving relationship, wherever there is relatedness, wherever there is a bond, sin is a painful affront. Were it not so the conclusion would have to be drawn that no real bond existed. It is precisely at this point—and this is an insertion for the theologically minded—it is precisely at this point that all those theories of the atonement which are couched in forensic terms, and in which the remission of the penalty plays a large part, are unsatisfactory. The judge is not related to the prisoner in the dock. He is not attached to him. He had not thought of him before the trial and he will not think of him again when the trial is over except perhaps in the club reminiscing with other judges over a glass of port. No, the relationship between God and you and me is more like that of a father and his beloved son, or a husband and his wife—and these are the images the Bible uses. In these relationships of love sin hurts terribly; if it did not love would be absent.

So because of the integrity of the moral law and the fact of divine love, forgiveness is bound to cost God. It could not be cheap. It could not be easy. There had to be an atonement; and once in history the evidence of its price was placarded up for all to see; it was the crucifixion of Christ. That poured out blood was for the forgiveness of sins, as witness my text for today from Ephesians 1.7: 'For in

Christ our release is secured and our sins are forgiven through the shedding of his blood.' The Cross of Christ guarantees the reality of God's forgiveness of our sins, if we confess them, if we repent. We must be careful never to stray from this, never to make it other than central in our worship.

We believe in the forgiveness of sins because of the Cross of Christ. This is where we are made one with God again, the broken fellowship restored. Or as T. Kelly expressed it in his hymn,

> The balm of life, the cure of woe,
> The measure and the pledge of love,
> The sinners' refuge here below,
> The Angels' theme in heaven above.

24. About Death

Beloved, we are God's children now; it does not yet appear what we shall be, but we know that when he appears we shall be like him, for we shall see him as he is.

1 JOHN 3.2 (RSV)

I don't really want to preach this sermon but I know I ought. I don't want to because the subject is all but taboo in today's conversation, and you know that what I am talking about cannot possibly be sex because everything to do with that subject is currently provided with the utmost publicity till we are wearied with it. Sex has become like chips with everything. No, I refer to death. Death is the great modern unmentionable. We draw a veil over it. We keep our funerals private and substitute a memorial service as more convenient. And as for funeral processions along the street led by a slow moving hearse, who can even remember them?

Yes, I am risking being dubbed 'morbid' by preaching this sermon, or even 'Victorian', than which is scarcely any description more contemptuous. And yet we all have to die. And in families, and among our friends, sooner or later death strikes, and when the deceased is dearly loved the hurt is terrible. Then not the least part of the terror is that the bereaved may be shunned by the community. He or she is an embarrassment. I have heard of people crossing to the other side of the street in order to avoid the encounter, the excuse being 'I wouldn't know what to say'. That is our trouble. We have shut the whole subject up in a box and dare not lift the lid. And so we have nothing to say. And, must I admit it, generally for decades the Christian pulpit, except perhaps at funerals when the mourners can 'take in' very little, the Christian pulpit has had nothing to say. This is why I am preaching this sermon. It cannot be right for the pastor to shepherd his sheep from the pulpit through all 'the changes and chances of this mortal life' *except one*, and that the greatest crisis of all, namely death, for fear of being dubbed 'morbid'.

1. *Where death is natural*

We all have to die. In this sense death is as natural as birth. Moreover it is not an event which takes place only at the end of life's span when the heart gives up; it begins to throw its shadow back to the twenties. There are sporting activities which are too demanding for the body after that age, pointing remorselessly to the time ahead when all sporting activities must cease. For fathers, facing up to the day when their sons can easily beat them at squash is a painful reminder that life is slipping away; so also for the pretty woman when the men start paying the attention to her daughter that they once paid to her. In one respect life is like a rocket. It shoots up into the sky with energy and thrust and then at its zenith begins to tail off, except that with us the tailing off process lasts longer and is more gradual. But we aren't at sixty-five what we were at fifty-five, and at seventy-five what we were at sixty-five. Holidays abroad cease, then holidays anywhere, till finally we are confined to our own garden, then to the house, then to one room, and then to our bed. What I am saying is this: death is a 'spread-out' affair, it does not only come at the end. We are already dying. To face this fact now, and it is a fact, is not morbid, it is realistic.

I said just now that death is a natural part of life. Yes, it is, but I do not think that the realization of this truth has in itself sufficient power to draw the sting of death; there is no gospel, no good news in it.

In 1984 there was published a novel by Elizabeth Webster entitled *A Boy Called Bracken*. It is a pretty story and I was much moved by it. It is about Jake, a high-powered Fleet Street journalist who, being warned that he had developed advanced leukaemia with only a few

105

months to live, retired to a cottage lent him in Gloucestershire where he might be quiet and think. And there, of all the unexpected events, a gipsy boy called Bracken befriended him. This boy possessed an uncanny sensitivity to the wild creatures of the countryside which led him to care for any he discovered wounded or hurt, nursing them back to activity and freedom. This skill he shared with Jake so that together they cared first for a kestrel with a broken wing and then for a badger pup bereft of its parents. So Jake's frenzied world of Fleet Street receded, being replaced by the world of nature with its normal rhythm of birth and death. Thus Jake came to see his own death as normal and accepted it peacefully. It is what we should all do. This anyway is the message of the book.

2. *Where death is unnatural*

As I have said I was impressed by the book and do not for a moment question the therapeutic value of living close to nature, but I do not think this remedy measures up to the hurt caused to human beings by the prospect of death. We are not animals; that is our glory, but it is also our liability. We cannot contemplate death calmly. Granted that for a few people death may come as a release from a burdensome existence but for most it is an offence, it breaks in as an unwanted intruder. We never grow accustomed to death.

Part of our trouble with death is that not only are we not animals, neither are we simply physical machines that wear out. Each one of us, over and above our physical body, has developed a distinctive personality partly conditioned by our body but not identical with it. Note the word 'developed' here. The personality I have, the personality you have, was not given at birth, but only the potentiality of it. Our distinctive personalities develop gradually as we live out our lives and react to the changing circumstances and challenges that come our way. Another way of expressing this is to say our individuality is being born as life progresses, and this goes on right to the last chapter of our consciousness. In the case of a human being then, as distinct from an animal, not only death but birth as well is spread over the whole of our conscious life; progressive death of the body, progressive birth of the personality. There is nothing new in what I am saying. St Paul was thoroughly aware of this when he wrote

106

to the Corinthians (2 Cor 4.16), 'Though our outer nature is wasting away, our inner nature is being renewed every day.'

Now because this is the truth about us as human beings we cannot be at ease about death. We are bound to ask if the apparent end of our outer nature is also the end of our inner nature. But where is the sense if this is so? Where is the sense in developing our individualities over the whole of our lives—and there is more to a seventy-year-old than there is to a seventeen-year-old—to have it rubbed out at the death of the physical body with which it is not identical? So the agonizing question asked long ago by Job in the Bible, 'If a man die shall he live again?' will not go away. We long for an answer and can never be at least peaceful about death until we find one, and we shall be disappointed if we look no further than the life/death, death/life rhythm we see in the world of nature for with human beings death is an offence.

3. *Life beyond nature*

Where then shall we look? I gather that some people today are finding assurance about life after death from the testimonies of the terminally ill who have been brought back from the jaws of death by resuscitation of the heart and who tell of the wondrous visions of a realm of light they have experienced. I do not doubt the genuineness of these testimonies. What is more, I cannot help but marvel that it is in the realm of medicine that cognizance is being given even to the idea of existence independent of the physical organism as its cause; because for a century it has been accepted as axiomatic medical thinking in Europe that, just as the whole world can be explained by the workings of physical and chemical forces, so can the human mind. There is nothing else. That climate of thought has so changed now that there is only professional research into the subject of life after death but also popular reporting of the testimonies of people who have been brought back to life through medical and surgical skill. None of us can fail to be interested in this, but I have to say that what these rescued people have experienced is not death but dying. I do not think these stories, impressive as they are, answer our question 'If a man die shall he live again?'

And there are those who allege that they have found evidence for survival after death from what, for instance, the Institute of Psychical Research, a learned and respectable body, is able to tell us; but it is disappointingly sketchy. Others look to the theory of reincarnation. This is unconvincing for the reason that our individuality is partly (I said 'partly') dependent on our physical body for its identity and it is difficult to see how, if we inhabited another body, we could be the same individual in the reincarnated state. So there is no immortality.

So I come back to the Christian faith. Yes, it is a faith and not a science, but it is not unreasonable. There is nothing at the end of the day to lighten the darkness of human death compared with the resurrection hope which is an essential part of the Christian Gospel. Christ is risen. Through faith in him we too shall rise. And our risen life will not mean a diffusion or reduction of our individuality but its fulfilment. Since it is apparently God's purpose that we should all be different from each other, to have that individuality blurred in the life to come could not square with that purpose. On the contrary our individuality, our personality will be enhanced or, to use a New Testament phrase, it will be glorified. It is true there has been no disclosure to us of what the conditions of that life will be, which being the case we must conclude that in the divine wisdom it is better that we should not know now; but we have this verse from the First Epistle of John (Chapter 3 verse 2): 'Beloved, we are God's children now; it does not yet appear what we shall be, but we know that when he appears we shall be like him, for we shall see him as he is.' What 'being like Christ' means is difficult, but of this we can be certain, our distinctive personality, our individuality will not only be retained, it will be enriched. This is *the light* in the darkness of death. It shines bright and clear from the resurrection of Christ. Take care that it is never lost from your vision. You need it. I need it. We all need it.

Other lights do not compare but are not to be despised in the dark days of bereavement. Other people have battled through and so must we, so can we. And when bereavement has hit us hard we can at least be thankful that the departed one has been spared the pain of the parting we are having to face. This is not much comfort but it is something. And this I read the other day. When someone we love has left us through the gate of death perhaps we could think of them saying, 'I have gone on ahead for a little while to greet those I love, and I know you love; you will catch up with me and we shall soon be together again. Don't cry too much, but don't be afraid to cry a little; I should be sorry if you didn't.'

25. Monotheism with a Difference

Once every year many clergymen in the Church of England—I cannot speak for the other Churches—used to go through an act of ducking. Perhaps they would invite a 'visiting preacher' to occupy their pulpit, or even go off for a short Whitsun holiday and let someone else 'take over'. (This killed two birds with one stone.) Or if the worst came to the worst, they took refuge by speaking about the Ordination Candidates' Appeal Fund. The Sunday of course was Trinity Sunday. They were not going to risk preaching on that subject! In short they ducked it. And if you think the modern Church has outgrown this inhibition I bid you notice in your Alternative Service Book that although a theme is suggested in Table 5 for every other Sunday in the Church's year, Trinity Sunday is left a blank. Moreover, whereas the Sundays following Trinity Sunday used to be labelled accordingly—first, second, third and so on, after Trinity—now they take their significance from Pentecost. So Trinity Sunday has lost its commanding place, and the description of God for which it stands receives little attention beyond the frequent repetition in public worship of the formula, 'the Father, the Son and the Holy Ghost (Spirit)'. Rarely, I suspect, is the Triune God preached.

And maybe you are thankful. Three persons in one God? What possible application can this have to the lives we live? God, plain and straightforward, yes maybe we can accept this idea. Christ, yes, as the teacher of Galilee—this we can comprehend. The Holy Spirit however is vague and little assisted by substituting 'Spirit' for 'Ghost'. And if all three are bound together and called God, indeed Three Persons in One God, we feel the time to take our leave has arrived. So how can the Trinity as a name for God find a place at all in the Christian Calendar?

1. *A puzzled Apostle*

Predominantly because it is implied in the pages of the New Testament. I said 'implied'. There is no doctrine of the Trinity specifically set out anywhere; and if you consult a Word Book of the Bible you will not even find the word 'Trinity' in the Index. The Trinity is not a Biblical phrase, which does not mean however that it is without roots in the New Testament; quite the reverse, and one of the most interesting places to see this is in the Gospel appointed to be

109

read on Trinity Sunday by the Alternative Service Book at the Eucharist.

It is about Philip, one of the twelve Apostles. Now Philip was a good man but a simple man, a man without subtlety in his thinking, a plain man, a man for whom black is black and white is white, a man to whose way of thinking one is one and three is three, they can't be anything else. He is Mr Average man. You can see Philip any day in the supermarket pushing one of those awkward barrows laden with food purchases for he helps his wife with the weekly shopping. A good man; but confront him with anything theological, let alone metaphysical, and he will leave you, scratching his head. How intriguing then on Trinity Sunday to be brought face to face with Philip puzzled in the Upper Room the night before Jesus his Master was crucified, because he could not figure out what on earth he was talking about; a puzzled Apostle, puzzled with doctrine. Doesn't that bring Philip close to you and me?

Philip is mentioned four times in the Gospels apart from the recording of his name in the lists of the Apostles, and all in St John, and on each occasion he is puzzled. First in Chapter 1 where it is encouraging to note anyway that Jesus chose a man like Philip to be an Apostle. Apparently we don't all have to be 'double firsts' to be called into Christ's service. But how lame, clumsy and woefully inadequate was Philip's description of his experience! 'We have met', he says, '*We* have met [I like that!] the man spoken of by Moses in the law and the prophets: it is Jesus, son of Joseph, from Nazareth.' Next time we see Philip (Chapter 6) scratching his head again trying to work out if twenty pounds would buy sufficient bread to feed five thousand people, a miracle never dawned on him. And next time (Chapter 12) we see him 'all in a dither' because he wasn't sure if some Gentiles who wished to meet Jesus would be received by him. And now in the fourth instance (Chapter 14) in the Upper Room the night before the crucifixion he heard Jesus say, 'If you knew me you would know my Father also. From now on you do know him; you have seen him.' But Philip's face was utterly blank.

The Father in heaven? Yes, he could follow that, he had always believed in God in heaven. But what is this about seeing the Father *in the man Jesus* standing before him? There can't be two God-the-Fathers! Poor Philip! Religion was becoming so complicated! 'Lord, show us the Father', he blurted out, 'and we shall ask no more.' At which Jesus must have sighed deeply for he replied, 'Have I been all this time with you, Philip, and you still do not know me? Anyone who has seen me has seen the Father. Do you not believe that I am *in the Father and the Father is in me*?' Poor Philip! One person in another person. What was Jesus talking about? Two modes of activity? God the Father, God the Son? No, he couldn't 'get it'.

And worse, as far as Philip was concerned, was still to come, for Jesus went on to say, 'And I will ask the Father and he will give you another Advocate who will be with you for ever—the Spirit of truth.' So God the Father, God the Son, God the Holy Spirit—the Trinity hinted at in the Upper Room the night before Jesus went forth to his crucifixion and resurrection—a revelation of the nature of God. Could Philip understand it? Can we understand it? But we ought to try, which is why Trinity Sunday still stands in the Calendar. But maybe it is a comfort to know that at first, perhaps always, one Apostle at least found the subject difficult, and we need not be too ashamed if, for a time anyway, we are left scratching our heads.

2. *Complex unity*

Do we believe then in three Gods? But in a moment we shall stand up and solemnly recite,

> We believe in one God, the Father,
>   the Almighty,
> Maker of heaven and earth,
> of all that is, seen and unseen.

This seems abundantly clear—one God. So we are monotheists, but—and this is the point for us—not monotheists like the Jews and followers of Islam. We believe in *three persons in one God*, only the word 'person' must be written with inverted commas because it does not refer to three separate individuals but to the three different ways of working of the one God—God as the Father, the creator of all that is; God working too as the Son of God, that is as Jesus Christ our Lord; and God working as the Holy Spirit, the Lord, the Giver of life.

Maybe an illustration will help; imperfect, I know, as I shall show in a minute, but not without value. Here is an artist, say Raphael. He creates in his mind that wonderful picture of the Madonna and Child; everything originates with that creative work of his. Without him and

111

without his thinking there would be no picture. To see it, however, there must be another mode of working other than thinking, so he takes a crayon and draws a cartoon. He is the same artist at work but he is working in another way. Nor is this all. We see him later on operating with a paintbrush, pigments and a canvas. He is still the same person but now he works as a painter. We could say then that Raphael was *three persons in one person*, provided we do not think of the word 'person' as meaning a separate individual.

An imperfect illustration of the Divine Trinity? Yes, of course, since the three modes of operation in the case of the artist succeed one another, whereas in the case of the Triune God, the three ways of God being God are eternal. This however should be sufficiently clear—unity, oneness is not a simple entity like the number one, it can be exceedingly complex; it is also more than the sum of the parts as is the case, for example, when we talk about the unity of a symphony, the one symphony operating at a number of levels.

But does it matter whether we believe or not that one can be complex and that our monotheism as Christians is *monotheism with a difference*? Some time ago I read in a book on the Trinity by Leonard Hodgson, published in 1943, of a discussion the author had with an Indian philosopher. It was all about our personal immortality. As the conversation proceeded it became clear that the Indian, who believed in the unity of God, was quite certain that if and when we shall ever be perfected beyond this mortal life it will be by absorption into the being of God, so we shall at last be rid for ever of our individual self-consciousness as will also all those whom we know and love. We—they—will be absorbed, lost in the ultimate unity of God which must comprehend everyone and everything. The Indian philosopher's way of thinking requires this. But our Christian monotheism is different. It is a complex unity; it believes in three persons in one God; it implies therefore differences in the oneness, and fellowship among the differences. Does this sound abstract? Of course it sounds abstract, but the meaning of it for us is that our individuality will not be lost when our earthly pilgrimage is over. On the contrary we shall become that for which we always had the potentiality. Fellowship with God and with one another is our final glorious destiny.

3. *A doctrine worth fighting for*

So do not write off the doctrine of the Trinity as unimportant. Rather it is the coping stone of our faith. It holds together what we believe, indeed what we experience. In all probability our religion became a living, personal reality for us at that time when we were moved by the wonder of something in nature such as a glorious summer morning, a landscape or an exquisite flower; or it could have been by the sheer goodness of someone we encountered; or some words in a book or spoken—possibly even by a preacher. We knew then that this was God addressing us. And then we moved on to recognize Jesus as the Christ, living, dying and rising again for us, and we knew that in encountering him we were encountering the same God. And then, thirdly, in the Christian congregation we know that it is different from the secular world because of its different Spirit, it is the Spirit of God, the Holy Spirit. And the likelihood is that we came to the Trinity in reverse, so to speak; first we encountered the Spirit in the Christian Church, then we learned of Christ, and then through him God became real to us. This is a truth the Eastern Orthodox Church has firmly grasped.

Do we take this lying down when we begin to see a glimmer of the truth for which the doctrine of the Trinity stands? But in the fourth century it had to be fought for, and the battle was in danger of being lost for Arius, a presbyter of Alexandria, was a doughty foe. Had he won the intellectual argument the Church would have surrendered to the idea of three gods, or a godhead in three tiers, the outcome of which would be a denial of Christ as giving a true picture of what God is like. A champion however rose up in the person of one called Athanasius, almost standing alone, hence the phrase connected with his name *Athanasius contra mundum*, Athanasius against the world. But he won in the end, and thank God he did. So now Christ can still be God for us. And there are not three Gods, not one God, hard and remote, but Three Persons in One God. Monotheism with a difference. No, we cannot wholly understand it. Who ever has understood it? Not even Athanasius, but he was right to contend for the Trinity, and so are we. Never let this doctrine go. In it is rooted our salvation and our hope. It is the coping stone of what we have come to believe through experience, and it is the foundation of our faith.

113

26. The Gift of Freedom

And he said, A certain man had two sons: and the younger of them said to his father, Father, give me the portion of thy substance that falleth to me. And he divided unto them his living. And not many days after the younger son gathered all together, and took his journey into a far country; and there wasted his substance with riotous living.

LUKE 15.11–13 (AV)

Unfortunately this is not an outdated story. I mean there must be parents today suffering agonies of mind when they discover the way some—I said 'some'—teenage sons and daughters of theirs are living now that they have left home. They have accepted as their due the inheritance of parental love, care, even of money given them and squandered it in life-styles that bewilder the older generation—all-night bottle parties, drugs and 'sleeping around'. Every now and again we read of some tragedy as a direct result of orgies such as these, and our hearts go out to the parents.

1. The father's problem

So it is of the father I want us to think in this parable of the Prodigal Son; not the son this time, but the father. Look at him. Look at him when his younger son comes asking for his share of the family money that will one day come to him. That younger son has no experience of life as yet beyond the family circle and those with whom it has chosen to associate. So what does he know about the fickleness of so-called friends? And how little of the fact that the only face you can see, or have a chance to read, is the one its owner chooses to turn towards you! There are sharks and twisters and slippery thieves, some of them most attractive, out to catch the innocent. Pity the father picturing his green boy adrift in that whirlpool of seductive men and women. What chance had he? Pity the father putting off his decision. Should he give the boy the money? Should he refuse it? Should he put up barriers so that the boy simply couldn't go? Should he cajole, threaten, even preach at him? All through the long night he tosses and turns on his bed knowing that next morning he must decide. What shall he do? What would you do? Well, this is what the father did. He gave the boy the money, the whole inheritance that would one day come to him, and *let him go*.

And now I see the father standing by his front gate saying goodbye to his departing boy and wishing him well. I can't believe the mother was not there too, and if I know anything about mothers, trying hard not to shed a tear and failing miserably. The trouble is, she loves that boy, the father loves him too, they both love him, every inch of him, immaturity and all. But they *let him go*. They stood watching him go, till he was but a dot on the distant landscape. They knew the terrible risk, but they let him go.

2. *Love needs freedom*

Now my question, a searching question. Would those parents have increased their boy's love of them if they had refused to let him go? Would there have been more love in the home, parents of child, child of parents, if they had tied him tight in their life-style? Would there not have been on the contrary resentment, moroseness and a large measure of secret rebellion? You know the answer. So do I.

A few days ago I heard of a wealthy Yorkshire coal owner, years ago now, who sent his eldest son to work in the pit so that he could learn the family industry from the bottom upwards. But the young man hated it. He hated every day of his life. The only bright spot was the girl in the tobacconist's kiosk at the corner of the street. And he fell in love with her, deeply in love. But the parents refused the marriage. She was only the girl in the tobacconist's kiosk at the corner of the street. So they refused to let him see her again. Are you surprised when I tell you that his life from then onward was an embittered, ruinous affair? They did not let him go.

3. *Freedom runs risks*

Let us grasp the point of all this. There can be no love unless there is freedom; and there can be no freedom which has no risks wrapped up in it. Loving someone does not mean safeguarding against the possibility—no, probability—of mistakes, even catastrophes. Love is always vulnerable.

So now perhaps we are in a position to raise the theological issue. Must not the love of God also run the risk of calamities and not

115

safeguard against them? Must not God also *let us go*, employing our brains, our skills, our technologies and our strengths, wherever they will lead us, even maybe into a dangerous far country?

On 6 August 1945 a device called 'Little Boy' containing significant material weighing only one twenty-eighth part of an ounce was dropped on Hiroshima, burning up 150,000 people in the terrifying explosion. Why did God ever allow Einstein thirty years previously to work out this fantastic equation, $E = mc^2$, making possible an atomic bomb? Why did God not block up the minds of the scientists so that they *could not* acquire this terrible skill? Why did he not strike them with paralysis, smash up their laboratories—anything to render impossible the awful risks involved? But no, God has let man ferret out the secrets of the universe as he will, so now we have nuclear missiles. He has let him go and put no security guard on the gate.

And the same kind of questions are raised about the appalling catastrophes that God allows in the world he is said to have created. A cyclone causing the Ganges Delta of Bangladesh to flood, drowning a million people. A failure of the monsoon south of the Sahara in Africa resulting in the slow starvation of hundreds of thousands of people because of the drought. These are mind-boggling numbers but the real poignancy is in the agony of all these as individuals, no way different from a baby born in a London hospital hideously deformed. Why does God allow this? Why does not God say to the force of nature as well as the forces of the human mind, 'Thus far and no further'? Why no barriers? Why does he let all this go?

4. *Three answers*

Let me try to give three answers, very briefly, perhaps too briefly.

First, no individual, no boy, no girl, no young man or young woman will ever grow up to maturity unless he is allowed to pit his strength and his skills against odds confronting him. If no odds, then no fully developed people. And God wants strong and wholesome people. So he lets people go.

Secondly, if fire did not always burn, if water did not always drown, if gravitation did not always operate, how could we live with such unreliability in nature? Of course the heart-rending tragedy is when the innocent suffer; when, for example, an electrical fault sets on fire the house of a bedridden woman living alone. No doubt sometimes miracles do happen, and remarkable escapes are 'in the news', but for the most part nature operates strictly according to the laws which govern it. Were it not so, we should all be 'at sea'. So God lets nature go.

Thirdly—and this seems strange so long as we forget the story of the father and the prodigal son with which I began this sermon—the father let the son go *because he loved him*, and because he wanted his love in return; and he knew this would never be if he kept him boxed up at home unable to try his wings. Of course the headstrong son ran into terrible trouble—debt, betrayals, brothels, disease (I shouldn't wonder), then destitution and hunger. But he came to his senses. Why? Because he knew that his father—and I must add his mother—still loved him, loved the wayward son, so loved that *they let him go* when he wanted his freedom.

And now the question—would the son have loved the father if he had refused to let him go? You know the answer. So here is the lesson for us all. Never doubt the love of God on the grounds that he does not strangle at birth tragedies happening in our world. He does not stop them because he loves. Do not forget this. Do not forget it when the going gets rough. Never doubt the love of God because it is always there. You can be sure of that. And so can I, hard as it is sometimes to understand, but we must try, we really must. At the end of the day we all depend on the love of God.